Step Out of the Box

YOUR DREAM LIFE IS WAITING

Step Out of the Box

YOUR DREAM LIFE IS WAITING

It is time to Erase & Replace the labels that are
keeping you from running YOUR race.

DIANA SUMPTER

XULON PRESS

Xulon Press
2301 Lucien Way #415
Maitland, FL 32751
407.339.4217
www.xulonpress.com

Printed in the United States of America.

ISBN-13: 978-1-54565-023-3

CONTENTS

HURRY INTO YOUR HIKING BOOTS;
IT'S TIME TO CHOOSE
THE PATH LESS TRAVELED

Have you ever woken up and realized the life you are living today is not the life you envisioned in your little girl dreams? That what started out as your dream life has become a nightmare? Maybe you've started to think you are exchanging the best years of your life for income instead of influence and impact. Are you using your gifts, talents, and abilities to build someone else's dream life instead of your own? Can you even remember the last time you woke up full of energy envisioning the day ahead as a treasure hunt instead of hunting for enough energy to just climb out of bed? What happened to our little girl dreams?

When we were little girls we dreamed big girl dreams, but now that we are big girls, we have settled for little dreams. Girlfriend, because you chose this book to read, I am positive there is a dream life hidden deep in your heart. It's the life you once dared to dream about as a little girl. It's the dream life that involved you making a difference in this big ole' world. That dream life where you were the Queen, the Princess, the CEO, Gold Medal Winner, Wife, Mom of the Year, and Wonder Woman all rolled into one. It's that life of endless possibilities where anything was possible.

You were once bold, brave, and some people even called you bossy. You knew you weren't bossy; you were born to lead! You had a vision and a purpose for your life that others couldn't see or even understand. Most likely, people laughed at this dream life of yours and shared with you all the reasons it was impossible to achieve. One day you started to believe the critics, and little by little you lost your way, little by little you settled, little by little you compromised. Time passed and life happened. You made some good and some not-so-good choices. Some things happened to you; some you could control, and some you could not. People said things about you, some were true and some were not. One morning you woke up and found yourself boxed in, living a life someone else designed for you. A life completely unlike the dream life you once envisioned.

My greatest wish is for you to live a life that energizes you and everyone around you. A life that finds you leaping out of bed saying, "Good morning, God!" instead of grumbling, "Good god it is morning!" This book will help you discover how you got here and to develop the tools you need to step into the most powerful version of yourself. Today you will begin living a life focused on thriving instead of surviving. Are you excited? Why not gather a few girlfriends around the table for the next couple of weeks, so you can help each other change the conversations in your head, which will ultimately change your legacy?

People—family, friends, and others whom you have not yet met—are waiting for you to be bold enough to achieve your dreams. They need your example to be the evidence they need to be brave enough to chase after their own dream life. In fact, until you break out of your box, they are as stuck as you are. There is a lot more on the line than you might realize. This book is all about equipping you to recognize why you are not living your dream life. To help you recognize then Erase and Replace the harmful thought patterns that are preventing you from living the life you were created to live.

Throughout our journey, we will step into the darkest corners of your mind to clean out cluttered thoughts and kick out that confused self-image. Then, looking through your rediscovered little-girl-anything-is-possible eyes, you will learn how to recognize and erase those Pitiful labels that are holding you hostage, so you can replace them with Powerful labels that will set you free. Free to live a life beyond your wildest dreams, a life of impact that will ripple across the globe for generations. Get ready to explore and leave behind living in the Land of the Lazy, maneuver out of the Maze of Mediocrity, then discover your dream life as you excel in the Land of Excellence! Along the journey ahead, you'll wear many different types of shoes. You'll need your Hiking Boots for the road less traveled,

Wedges to find the places where fear is holding you hostage, House Shoes for cleaning and redecorating your thoughts, Rain Boots for battling life's storms, Combat Boots to win the daily thought battle, Tennis Shoes for running away from regret, and finally, High Heels to step into your dream life in the Land of Excellence.

POWERFUL AND PITIFUL LABELS

Powerful labels are in a constant war with Pitiful labels. Powerful labels say, "I can do this," and "I am different than others because I have a different calling." Pitiful labels are words that hold you hostage in a box created by fear and unworthiness. Words like, "I can't do that," or "I'm not like them." To be successful, it is necessary to dig deep and listen carefully to your often-overlooked mind chatter. It's important to recognize the words flying around in that pretty head of yours all day long. It will make the difference between living a life of excellence and spending your life meandering in the Maze of Mediocrity.

It is important to recognize these words are labels that represent your self-identity. Your self-identity is who you believe you are and what you believe you can accomplish. Your life is unique. The set of circumstances in which you've lived combined with your experiences and what people have said about you have shaped your identity. How you perceive yourself and others, and why you are living within your current set of circumstances, is a direct reflection of your identity.

My friend Sean Key says in his leadership coaching sessions, "You can only outrun your identity for so long." When people see themselves differently than how they are performing, a reset will

10

occur. Everything seems to be going along fine, and then, out of nowhere, there is an internal switch from success to self-destruct. This self-destruct mode will stay in place until the success level again matches the identity. The only solution to break this "stop and go" cycle is to the change the thought patterns associated with the cycle. No matter how hard you work, you will reset every time you get too far from your self-identity.

Your identity works like a thermostat. A thermostat controls the temperature in a room. Once set, it controls the equipment to make the temperature match the regulated temperature. Your identity works the same way. When your success level is set at five and you start performing at an eight, your thermostat (self-identity) kicks in by creating a diversion of some sort that causes you to revert back to level five success.

That sounds crazy doesn't it? But it happens all the time. Someone comes into a business and is soaring to the top, then they start to make unwise business decisions, begin having personal issues, mismanaging their time and money, and partnering with the wrong people. Before too long, they start to lose momentum, fear sets in, and they start playing "not to lose" instead of "playing to win." They will tumble downward to the point that their self-identity is equal to their position on the scoreboard. This is why personal growth is so important. Top performers invest a lot of time and money into personal growth opportunities. It is a constant battle between where you are destined to go and where your self-identity believes you can achieve. This is the box—your box. The one that keeps your success at level five when you are really a level ten kind of girl!

Throughout this book you will find Excellence in Action exercises to help you learn to recognize unhealthy thoughts and replace them so you can change the way you see yourself. This is how you pivot into the most powerful version of your life. Here is the first exercise:

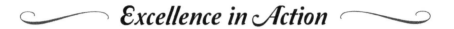

Excellence in Action

Make a list of the top three Pitiful labels you use to describe yourself:

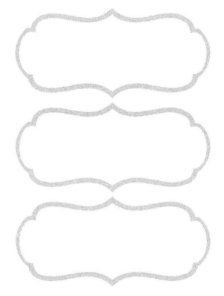

We are going to Erase and Replace these thoughts more in the next chapter, so keep writing new self-descriptive words down as more come to mind. Maybe even ask your close friends or family members what they think you believe about yourself. Also think about where you picked up this unhealthy description of yourself. This is a real Be Brave challenge! Look for common statements between what you think of yourself and what family members and friends hear you speak about yourself (not what they think about you). Their input will give you a full-circle vision of your self-identity. Like it or not, this is who you think you are, and it will determine how you will live the rest of your life.

Now, picture yourself standing in a box. Everything you desire, the life you dream of living, is just outside your reach. No matter how much you work or how hard you work, you cannot stretch far enough to reach it. No matter how bad you want to reach it, your dream life is unreachable. It is so close and yet so far away.

PROFIT

PASSION

POSITION

PEOPLE

PLATFORM

PURPOSE

SELF-IDENTITY

Keep in mind this crazy box wasn't created overnight. It was created when life's demands, disappointments, and delays started to take their toll on your dreams, when the voices of your critics grew louder and louder, and as your victories became further and further apart. It happened slowly, but as you started to believe the Pitiful labels "You're not good enough" or "I'll never make it" your identity started to develop into someone you don't recognize. Your identity was hijacked every time a new Pitiful label was placed on your back. With every new Pitiful label you unknowingly accepted, you stepped further into your box, and eventually, you found yourself buried in those Pitiful labels.

I often wondered why I sometimes felt powerful and at other times I felt pitiful. I could always appear powerful. When I was in the Air Force, I was selected to serve in a special-duty assignment. I declined it because of the travel requirements and, due to my high-level security clearance, I could not tell my family where I was going or what my job entailed. However, the following Monday morning I found myself reporting to that assignment. My official title became a "non-volunteer for a volunteer special-duty assignment." The men I worked with were not used to working with a woman, and especially not a strong, know-it-all 21-year-old. For the first time in my life, I met a boss I immediately disliked, and he felt the same way about me. When our two egos and faith differences were added to the mix, it was a recipe for disaster. During this time, I accumulated many not-so-flattering labels. When the two of us were in the same room, the tension was unmistakable. Quickly, I realized this could not be the life I was designed to live. He tried hard to give me the "You're bossy" label. "No," I corrected, "I'm a leader."

Have you ever been misunderstood? It is so frustrating; isn't it? I was labeled "bossy", a label I have fought my entire life because I step up to take the lead if no one is leading with excellence. People seem to want to follow me because I genuinely care about what we are accomplishing together and who they are becoming in the process.

When someone says my granddaughter Dakota is bossy, I make sure I take a deep breath before my "Military Me" takes over and rips their head off. I just smile nicely and very quietly say, "She is not bossy at all; she is a leader, and I can't wait to see how God will use her in the future. Isn't that fun to think about?" I've never received pushback for sharing that, and the best part of all is that Dakota hears me speaking truth into her life. I speak up because I don't want anyone to squash her leadership ability and place labels on her that could prevent all the amazing things God has in store for her life. The gifts and talents she is displaying in childhood and adolescence will be the same gifts and talents needed to fulfill her purpose. So as moms, grandmas, aunts, sisters, and girlfriends, we have to protect our kids from those labels that can keep them boxed in from the life they were designed to live.

I have found that most people don't realize their life is controlled by their most prevailing thoughts. It doesn't matter if the prevailing thoughts are good or bad, because the subconscious doesn't know if what is said is a lie or the truth. Your subconscious manifests everything you tell it to create in your life. Did you know there is a part of the brain called the Reticular Activation System (RAS)? The RAS is the part of your brain that serves as a filter between your conscious mind and your subconscious mind. The RAS, which is located in the core of your brain stem, takes instructions from your conscious mind, and passes them onto your subconscious mind. Because of this biological function, whatever you are thinking about or focusing upon will seep into your subconscious mind only to reappear at a future time.[1]

Have you ever decided that you wanted to buy a certain car, then all of a sudden you start to see the car you wanted everywhere? That is how the RAS works. For example, if you want happy, appreciative, fun people in your life, make a list of these qualities, tape the list on every mirror in your house and watch how your RAS finds those types of people. What you talk about, you bring about! Napoleon Hill taught us that "Whatever your mind can conceive and believe the mind can achieve regardless of how many times you may have failed in the past."[2] This hidden secret power of the mind has been around for a long time. The Bible talks about this in Philippians 4:8:

> Finally, beloved, whatever is true, whatever is honorable, whatever is just, whatever is pure, whatever is pleasing, whatever is commendable, if there is any excellence and if there is anything worthy of praise, think about these things. (NIV)[3]

If you want happy, well-mannered, others-focused kids, then speak them into existence. Our granddaughter, Dakota, is one of the happiest human beings on the planet. We constantly speak this into her life and recognize her gift of encouragement and her positive outlook. I knew we had securely planted this seed of "happy" in her heart when we had to go to the hospital because she was covered with some kind of skin rash. As we were walking up to the hospital door holding hands, she looked up at me and said, "Nana, I just can't find a smile to give out today. Can you give out the smiles today?" My eyes welled up with gratitude for such a sweet spirit in this precious girl, and I told her I would be honored to give out the smiles today, and she could take over tomorrow.

Contrast that to a plane ride I was on earlier this year with two girls under five seated behind me. For the entire ride, the youngest child kicked my seat and cried. When we landed, I looked back at the mom, who was exhausted from trying to calm this child down. I wanted to give her some encouragement, so I said to the other child, "You did a great job on the flight." This little girl looked me straight in the eye and said, "Yes, I was good because the first child is always good and the second one is a troll." Oh my, that entire family had created a troll in this second child; she was just living out their expectations. What labels are we putting on our kids and grandkids? You will harvest what is planted in their lives. Girlfriend, let's choose wisely.

POWER OF A PIVOT

Since we choose the thoughts we believe, let's make sure what we are saying both out loud and inside our head aligns with the results we want to happen in life. Words repeated often enough determine our choices. Over time, seemingly inconsequential daily choices become big choices, and these choices determine how you will interact with family, friends, coworkers, and the strangers around you. If you make choices based in the truth of Powerful labels, you can conquer the world. If your decisions are based on the lies of Pitiful labels, you are a slave to the world. The choice is yours: either exert power over your life, or life will exert its power over you.

Your words and thoughts influence your legacy every day. How empowering is that? Just think, a one-degree pivot in thinking alters your whole legacy, regardless of the external influences in your life! The key to having power over your life is understanding what labels are, how they influence what we think of ourselves, and how they determine the decisions we make. Jim Rohn once related that

The choice is yours: either exert power over your life, or life will exert its power over you.

neither a marriage nor a business fails overnight. Cataclysmic failure generally comes from a series of small, correctable failures. He calls these failures "one-degree failures.[4]"

Let's look at the power of a one-degree pivot. If you were flying from New York to Los Angeles, and your course was off by just one degree, you would need to pull out that flotation device the flight attendants are always talking about, because you would land in the Pacific Ocean! I have a friend named Matt who is a retired Air Force pilot. He shared an interesting fact about flying: every single degree you fly off course will cause you to miss your target landing spot by about 92 feet for every mile you fly. This amounts to about a mile off target for every 60 miles flown. So, the longer you travel off course, the farther away you will be from your intended target. That's why the pilot and the autopilot are constantly checking the course and making adjustments. This is exactly how you get out of your box. You and your auto pilot (your subconscious) have to work together to pivot those thoughts and words to put you on the right path to your dream life.

There does come a time in your life where you are so buried in Pitiful labels that you have to work to remember a time you were powerful. Remember that time when you were at the top of your game? It might have been a while ago, but there was a time when you were powerful beyond compare, when everything in your life just clicked. When you are operating with Powerful labels, you created high levels of motivation, momentum, expectations, results, and creativity in your life! You attracted successful, fun people who wanted to partner together to create positive change. Then, little by little, you pivoted away from these daily success habits that created this "Power Zone" because a one-degree deviation in your head, heart, habits, health, or amount of help you have in place, can throw you way off course.

DESIGNING YOUR DREAM LIFE

You have to figure out what makes you tick; what makes your soul sing, and what makes your heart race. These will light the path to defining and achieving your dream life. When your natural gifts are combined with your passion, great things happen. Once you know where you're headed, on a day-by-day basis, you can work to create your dream life one small choice at a time.

Girlfriend, hurry into those Hiking Boots! We need to pivot onto the right path to your dream life. This path will take you to the deepest part of your heart to find where stepping stones have become stumbling blocks and where blessings have become burdens. It is all in how you frame a choice, a conversation, or a conflict. When you are equipped with your Hiking Boots, you can choose the path less traveled to your dream life. Are you ready to start?

Excellence in Action

Take your first step by beginning to design your dream life by answering these questions:

 What brings you joy?

 What are your gifts and talents?

 When have you felt the most powerful?

 If you had plenty of money and did not have to work your current job, what would you do with your time?

 If success was guaranteed, what would your dream life look like in five years? Ten years? Twenty-five years?

Your answers to the questions above hold the answers to designing your dream life. It is unfortunate that most people don't invest the time or energy to determine what is important to them. Instead, they spend their entire lives complaining about circumstances. Most people spend more time designing a dream vacation than they do designing a life of their dreams. They are life's victims, but not you, my friend, you are a victor. But in order to experience victory, you have to know the starting point of your race; what lane you will run in, and what the finish line looks like.

Are you starting to remember some of your little girl dreams yet? I sure hope so! God was not joking with you about those dreams. What God originates, He orchestrates. He is faithful, so He would not lay all of these hopes and dreams on your heart and then say, "Ha, ha, just kidding!" Whatever your dream, God has given you a glimpse of what He has in store for you along with the purpose for your life. He has also equipped you with the gifts, talents, and abilities to make it happen. However, you have to do the work to find the purpose, which will produce the passion, and when purpose and passion are mixed with Powerful labels, anything is possible! (Yes, that is a lot of "P" words!)

Excellence in Action

Here are a few more questions to equip you to define your dream life:

 What would my life look like if I could be, do, have anything, or go anywhere?

 Who or what organizations would I bless financially, if money was not an issue?

 What kind of life is waiting on me when I step out of this box?

 Who would be positively impacted internally, externally, and eternally when I step out of this box?

Now that you have a more clear vision of your dream life, write down a few of the most important aspects of your dream life in the lines outside of the box below:

DREAM LIFE
(CHAPTER 1)

SELF-
IDENTITY

Remember the saying "If nothing changes, then nothing changes?" It's true. Today is the day you make a change in the trajectory of your life. Just think of the power you will give those around you to be brave, to think a new thought, to change an entire generation, because their dreams are connected yours.

This cramped three-by-three box is preventing you from stepping into your sixteen-by-twenty dream life. You, my sweet friend, were never designed to live in this box. You can step out of it anytime you want. I believe the majority of the population will spend their entire lives living in their box without even realizing it. They have become programmed to settle or—even worse—to quit. They can't see how close they are to living the life they were called to live. But not you; you know you don't belong in that box.

Did you know that you are much closer to living your dream life than you think? Only a few pivots here and some new labels there will lead you to living the life of your dreams. Hurry into your Hiking Boots, we are going to follow the path that takes you straight to your dream life! This is truly exciting. You will need a few tools for this journey, so in the next chapter you will discover how to take on the negative people in your life. Turn the page, and get ready to sparkle!

Women of Excellence

OPAL GAIL JOHNSON

Our mom was diagnosed with Chronic Severe Rheumatoid Arthritis (RA) when she was only 49 years old (the diagnosis came only three months after I left home). She and Dad had always talked about how they wanted to travel when Dad retired and my sister Donna and I were out of the house. Their dream life was just beginning. One week she was bowling three times a week and the next she could barely move her hands or walk. Her labels of "super mom, wife, cook, hostess" came from her ability to run an immaculate household. When RA overtook her body, her life shifted. Not only did the pain and destruction from the disease overtake her body, it also shifted her entire identity. She could not do anything with her hands, which meant no cooking, cleaning, gardening, or decorating without help.

Mom and Dad were married when she was 16 years old. They married on a bet and remained married until she passed 54 years later. As she followed Dad around the world during his Air Force career, she discovered her talent for cooking and hospitality. She could whip up a dinner for eight without a dirty dish to be seen and not break a sweat. We marveled at her every holiday, as she made it look so easy. We appreciate it even more now that we are in charge of that task. To this day, we have never figured out how stay ahead of those dirty dishes!

Mom chose to work the morning shift at local restaurants, so she would be home every afternoon when I got home from school. The woman I am today came from the time we spent together talking about school and the angst of being a teenage girl every afternoon while we got dinner ready for Dad. She was my best friend and confidant. I could tell her anything because we spent so much one-on-one undistracted time together. Her family was her career, and she lived it with excellence. The greatest gifts she and Dad gave us girls are roots and wings. Dad told us we could do anything, and Mom loved us no matter the choices we made. This allowed us to be ridiculously brave in life.

I remember coming home on leave from the Air Force and sitting up with her as the pain radiated through her little body. Still she never complained. Never once did we hear her say "Poor me" or "I am a rheumatoid arthritic." She never let her disease become her label. RA was the disease she had, but it never became who she was. She got every day and put on her makeup, met with a group of ladies for coffee, and she and Dad went out to eat most nights. They chose to focus on what they could do not what they could not do because Mom refused to wear her disease as a label. She always reminded us to never wait on your dream life, live full out today, because it can all change overnight. Don't let life define who you are, regardless of your health, be it good or bad. Let the way you choose to live your life define who you are and how you are remembered.

FIND YOUR FILTER AND GLITTER; IT'S TIME TO PUT THE RIGHT TOOLS IN THE TOOLBOX

One of the most important lessons to learn right away is this: not everyone you share your dream life with will understand your newfound enthusiasm for life. They will try to talk you right back into your box. "Don't get your hopes up too high," they'll say. "I don't want you to be disappointed." Their motives are good, but sometimes you just have to love them where they are and say, "Bless their little heart."

In the south, we use this term a lot. When we are thinking, *What an idiot. Why did she do that?* out loud we say, "Bless her heart; she is just doing the best she can!" This statement might seem negative until you realize that people really are doing the best they can! Their decisions and choices are based on personal experiences, what they have seen modeled, and the labels through which they perceive the world.

Approaching conversations from this "Bless her heart" perspective will allow you to show much more grace and mercy to those around you. Saying (or thinking), "I would never do that!" should throw up a red flag in your mind that reminds you to observe this situation from the other person's perspective. Chances are, if you had the same personality, background, and life experiences, you would probably make the same choices they are making.

This knowledge is a game changer because it helps you work with all types of people without going crazy or hurting their feelings. Instead of "Bless their little hearts" being a negative statement, it now becomes a tool to show grace. This change in perspective removes a lot of the drama from your life because you will quit trying to make people respond to a situation the same way you would. This game of control is exhausting for all involved. You get to decide how you handle this particular confrontation.

You can look at the situation from a reaction mode by asking, "Why does she do that?" OR you can look at the situation from a responding mode and ask instead, "I wonder what is going on in her life that is causing her to make that choice?" These two questions even feel different, don't they? You might have even felt a difference in your body language as you read through those questions. Can you imagine the difference in your life when you move from being reactive to being responsive? This change in response allows you to move forward on your own journey while giving the other person the freedom to do the same.

CONQUER THE CHAOS

I carried this lesson into working with people in all areas of my life and added in my secret ingredient: a can of spray glitter! When someone makes an unwise decision, doesn't do what they said they would do, or are just rude, I put my hand over my heart and say out loud, "Bless her little heart; she is just doing the best she can," and then I spray myself with glitter. If someone at the church hurts your feelings, say a prayer, and spray yourself with glitter. If someone at your job wants to quit, wish the best for her, find her replacement, and spray yourself with glitter! It is impossible to be sad or mad when you are covered with glitter.

It is impossible to be sad or mad when you are covered with glitter.

Contact me at www.DianaSumpter.com the first time you get to use your glitter and let me know how powerful you feel.

Most of my life, I did not play well with others—especially

females. In high school, I was not interested in normal girly activities. Instead of trying out for the cheerleading team, I kept the stats for the football team. I was on the sidelines with the guys wearing jeans, not in a cheerleading outfit. My whole life I was told I was the son my dad never had. While my sister helped our mom in the kitchen, I hauled hay with the guys, helped Daddy with his business, or worked on our farm.

At every turn, people spoke this label into my life. Then, not realizing the limitation of this Pitiful label, I went out to prove them correct. Anytime I was involved with females it was a train wreck. They cried, they whined, they griped, and I could not understand why they did not just find the solution and do something about their problems. So, I took it upon myself to tell them how weak and stupid they were acting. I thought I was doing them a favor. Silly me, it's no wonder I did not have any friends! This Pitiful label is the reason I turned down a college scholarship opportunity to instead join the Air Force at age 17, just two weeks after graduating high school. I told my recruiter I wanted a job where no females were around, so he placed me in the telecommunications field.

In 1981, the year I joined the Air Force, telecommunications was a budding industry and very few females had entered the sector. Until I was 23 years old, any relationship or career decision I made was through my "You don't work well with females" label. It was from this filter that I made all decisions. If an event or opportunity involved a lot of women, I stayed away from it at all costs, whether it was social, church, or work.

Have you ever found yourself at a place in life where you knew the decisions you were making were not healthy for your priorities or peace of mind, but you did not know how to escape? Have you ever been on a path that was taking you down a road you did not really want to travel, but everyone around you told you that was where you belonged? Well, that was me at 23 years old. Back then, I had no friends, debt, and chaos in every area of my life. One of my life's greatest lessons was shared by a great friend and mentor, Connie Lamp. She taught me, "When chaos is present in more than one area of your life, look in a mirror to find the source of the problem."

This life of chaos and confusion was the one I once lived. I knew my marriage could be much better. I knew I could be a much better mom, but everyone kept telling me I was where I was supposed to be. I knew I was supposed to impact people in a positive way but had no idea how that could ever happen. How do you positively impact people if you don't like them? Every day, I would wake up and put on that Pitiful label "You don't work well with women," and "You are just one of the guys" and go to work knowing this was not the life that God designed me to live. Does any of this sound familiar?

 # Excellence in Action

Take a second and jot down a few areas in your life where there is chaos, conflict, or confusion:

_____

_____

_____

Maybe it is time to see if there is common ground between these areas. Ask yourself:

- Does the need to prove yourself good enough create chaos in your relationships?

- Is being right all of the time causing conflict in your relationships?

- Have you looked at these confusing situations through the other person's perspective?

These three questions helped me evaluate how I could communicate with other people differently. We cannot change others, but we can change how we communicate and respond to certain situations.

Looking back, my real problem was my low self-esteem and lack of communication skills. I grew up in a household that valued being right more than protecting someone's feelings or seeing another's perspective. I believed my well-developed debating skill—always focused on being right—was a valued strength, and the military fueled this habit and label. Over time I learned that saying whatever is on your mind without a filter is not always a good thing to do.

I had to learn to engage my Jesus Filter. You can name your filter whatever you like, based on your religious beliefs, but this is what I call mine. My Jesus Filter helps me to listen to people through the filter of curiosity and not condemnation. It allows me to ask myself: *I wonder why they are acting like that?* Instead of thinking: *How dare them! How stupid of them! I would never do that!* This filter, along with a can of glitter, has added years to my life by eliminating emotional drama. Now friendships are based on mutual respect, acceptance, understanding, and grace. My friend, are you being boxed in with chaos, confusion, and conflict? If so, maybe it is time to look in the mirror and evaluate your part in this crazy life you are living. Start looking at people through the eyes of compassion and find some common ground. Evaluate whether your frustration is really coming from the people around you or if it is a consequence of living somebody else's idea of your dream life.

ERASE AND REPLACE

Now that we have some tools in place to protect ourselves from what others think, feel, and say about our dream life, let's start working on replacing your Pitiful labels with Powerful labels. As you erase the Pitiful labels and replace them with those Powerful labels, you will begin to step out of your box. Labels are a personal perception of our life experiences and conversations. Labels are emotions, they are how we feel when we think about a situation or conversation. Those emotions are determined in our heart and not our head. We are not talking about logical, rational thinking; we are talking about the "I need to eat a whole tub of ice cream" kind of thinking. Let me show you how to Erase and Replace a label based on the same experience in either a Powerful or Pitiful thought:

PITIFUL	REPLACE	POWERFUL!
I am the dumb one.		*I am the smart one.*
I am the unlucky one; if something bad can happen, it will happen to me.		*I am the lucky one; only good things happen to me.*
This is not what we do in our family.		*I love being a trailblazer, how exciting to be the first in my family to reach this type of goal.*
I am the wrong color; I am too tall; too short; I am from the wrong country; etc.		*I am beautifully and wonderfully designed.*

Do you recognize any of them? I bet you have some others that are coming to mind. Let's take a second to write down some of the Powerful and Pitiful labels you deal with on a daily basis. Writing them down along with where you first recognized this label in your life will allow you to reframe Pitiful labels into Powerful labels. I call this doing an "Erase and Replace." This activity is so much fun because you get to own the emotion instead of the emotion owning you.

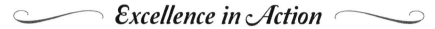

Excellence in Action

In the labels below, list your Pitiful labels and a brief reminder of where you picked up the label.

Now let's do an Erase and Replace on your Pitiful labels:

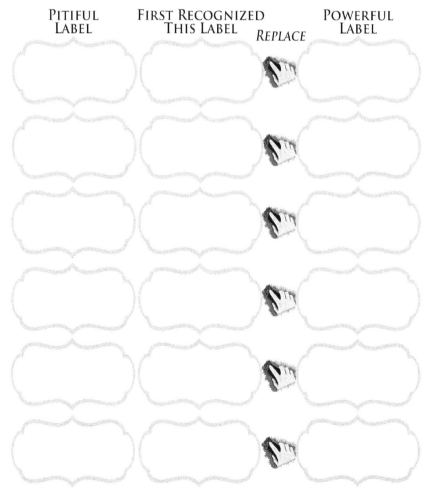

PITIFUL LABEL	FIRST RECOGNIZED THIS LABEL	REPLACE	POWERFUL LABEL

Let's look at some other labels that might have begun as a poor choice you made and later regretted. Maybe someone called you a name, or maybe you gave that name to yourself; either way, it became attached to your identity. These types of labels are the most dangerous because we judge ourselves by what we did instead of who we were wonderfully and beautifully designed to be.

All labels can change the entire trajectory of your life because, if allowed, they will alter your belief system. When your belief system changes from Powerful to Pitiful, it impacts your ability to choose wisely. Your focus is now on the fear of failing or looking foolish instead of being bold or brave. This fear stops you from purposefully moving ahead toward your dreams. You say, "no" to each opportunity that presents itself. Sometimes your internal voice speaks up and says, *Not now, there's something else I need to do*, because you don't feel like you can live up to someone else's expectations. Both "no" and "not now" are signs you are comfortable in that silly box of limitations. You may not even realize the opportunities you passed by were your first step out of the box and onto the road leading to your dream life. Yikes!

That one choice of saying "yes" will be the first step down the path to your dream life, whether it is starting the business you've always wanted, starting a community group at church, starting reconciliation of a broken relationship, losing weight, or anything else you are feeling called to create. When you choose faith over fear, hope instead of hurt, or motion over emotion, you will pivot yourself right out of that box.

Girlfriend, can you remember how powerful you were before you lived your life in that Pitiful box? Are you sick and tired of living a life that someone else decided you should live, trying to make everyone happy and trying to be perfect all of the time, all the while…

- knowing this life just doesn't feel right.

- knowing there is a life beyond the walls of this box that is waiting for you to be brave enough to step out from under those Pitiful labels.

- knowing that being bold enough to step out would inspire so many others to do the same.

- knowing there are organizations and missions waiting for you to have the money to invest in them, so they can live out their dream life of serving others.

Excellence in Action

Ask yourself: "What negative labels or beliefs are holding me back?" Write the Pitiful labels on the lines below.

Now ask yourself: "What positive labels or beliefs are moving me in the direction of my dream life?" Write down the Powerful labels on the lines below.

Remind yourself of the dream life you envisioned from chapter 1.

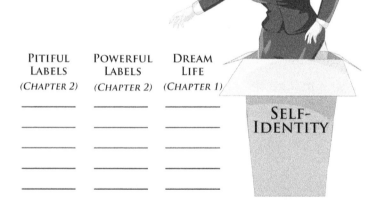

PITIFUL LABELS (CHAPTER 2)	POWERFUL LABELS (CHAPTER 2)	DREAM LIFE (CHAPTER 1)	SELF-IDENTITY
___	___	___	
___	___	___	
___	___	___	
___	___	___	
___	___	___	

Take a picture of this box with your phone and save as your wallpaper or print it and tape it to your mirror to remind you of the dream life waiting on you based your daily choices.

Growth Through Gratitude

Each day, write in your gratitude journal whether your day was driven by Pitiful or Powerful labels. You'll find an Erase & Replace Gratitude Journal starting on page 159 of this book. You can start today to build a new habit. (For more journal pages, you can go to www.dianasumpter.com for a free download of the "Erase & Replace Gratitude Journal.")[5]

When there is more Pitiful than Powerful happening in your head, put your Jesus Filter on and grab that can of glitter. It is easy to be grateful for the growth when you are covered in grace and glitter!

It is easy to be grateful for the growth when you are covered in grace and glitter

Women of Excellence

MARY KAY ASH

When I think about living an abundant life of choosing Powerful labels over Pitiful labels, the first woman I think of is Mary Kay Ash. I had the privilege of meeting Mary Kay Ash when I was 24 years old. I sat in her home and listened to her speak. I was moved by her vision, inspired by her wisdom, and motivated to live a powerful life because of her example. What I admired the most was her resilience, no matter what life threw her way, she chose to look for the lessons to be learned, and she focused on the positive aspects of every situation. She chose to live life outside the box. On Mary Kay's birthday this past year, my sister Donna and I put together this list of words that described how we saw Mary Kay living her life. Here is what we saw, and we challenge you to live a life that chooses:

Audacious instead of Afraid

Breakthrough instead of Breakdown

Courageous instead of Cowardly

Determined instead of Discouraged

Empowered instead of Enabled

Faithful instead of Fearful

Go-Giver instead of Go-Getter

Hopeful instead of Hyped up

Integrity instead of Indifference

Joyful instead of Jaded

Knowledgeable instead of Knocked Down

Liveliness instead of Laziness

Magnificent instead of Mediocre

Noteworthy instead of Nobody Cares

Opportunities instead of Obstacles

Powerful instead of Pitiful

Quality instead of Quantity

Relentless instead of Remorseful

Selfless instead of Selfish

Thoughtful instead of Thoughtlessness

Uncommon instead of Uniformity

Victor instead of Victim

Winner instead of Whiner

Xtra-ordinary instead of X-actly like everyone else

Yearn instead of Yield

Zealous instead of Zapped

WIGGLE INTO YOUR WEDGES; IT'S TIME TO STEP OUT IN FAITH AND REMOVE THE WEDGE OF FEAR

Remember the Angry Bird (™) craze? One day, our granddaughter Dakota was playing this game on my cell phone, and I asked her to teach me how to play. Immediately, she launched into an informative lecture worthy of a professor. Once she finished giving instructions along with tips on how to successfully play the game, she handed me her phone for a chance to play. Dakota laughed as I sat there confused, just staring at the game on the screen. Then, in an exasperated nine-year-old tone, she said, "Nana, do something I just taught you!" I asked. "How? I can't get off start. You taught me everything but the most important step!"

It dawned on me that this is also true for all of us who are coaches, mentors, or leaders of any organization. We have systems, processes, and checklists. We understand the need for personality and gift tests and what we need to do to make people feel loved and appreciated. We know how the win will feel. We have visualized it. We have created the call list to start the charity, fill volunteer teams, or grow the business, and yet we just stare at that 500-pound phone with every negative thought imaginable running through our heads.

We don't know how to get off start. We don't know how to remove the Wedge of Fear standing in the way of our vision and mission.

Aren't you sick of fear holding you hostage in that box, weighed down with limiting labels? Can't you feel the sense of urgency? People are waiting on you to make a difference!

Grab a cup of coffee, and wiggle into your Wedges. We're going on a journey to wedge deep into your heart and mind to discover the places fear is holding you hostage in the land of "What if…" and "If only…" In this place, residents are bound by the fear of failure, fear of success, fear of rejection, fear of approval, fear of making the wrong decision at the right time, or making the right decision at the wrong time. The fear list goes on and on.

As long as you remain wedged between faith and fear, you cannot live out your God-ordained life vision.

As long as you remain wedged between faith and

fear, you cannot live out your God-ordained life vision. (Because we all know how uncomfortable it is to have a wedgey, today we are going to get ourselves straightened out and step out in faith!)

After eight years in the Air Force and 30 years in business, I have found "If only" is one of the most dangerous phrases in the human language. You are telling the people in your life they are not enough. That "If only" you had a better man, a better job, a different title, a bigger house, more kids, fewer kids, better health, a better body, better pastor, etc., your life would be fulfilled. Because you are so focused on the lack, you cannot appreciate the abundant blessings you have in your life right now.

My mentor, Karen Piro, explains this beautifully: "Pleasantly dissatisfied is the point in your life where you realize there will always be more to attain, but you choose to be peaceful during the process." This is where we choose not to confuse our self-worth with the scoreboard, family situation, or weight on the scale. We realize true success is discovering the person we are becoming in the process is more important than the goal we are achieving. This is the tension between the panic-driven life we live today and the purpose-filled life we were designed to live.

Too often we hope and wish to start this great business, ministry, or charity, and we talk about the difference we are going to make in this world. Then the "If onlys" start. If only I had more money, more people, a different marital status, etc. The list goes on and on. If you cannot take care of the blessings and assignments you have now, you will not be trusted with more. If you can't handle 1,000 dollars a month, then you cannot handle 10,000 dollars. If you can't handle a group of 50, then you cannot handle 500. So what is the answer? GET OFF START! Master what you have right now; find your strengths, and delegate your weaknesses.

You might be thinking: *How do I know what strengths I have?* A strength is something that comes easily to you. You learn it quickly; it brings you joy, and you can see yourself doing this "thing" for the rest of your life. Put all of your resources into your strengths, so you can master them, and pay others to do the things not included in your strengths. For example, I partner with my sister, Donna. She is one of the most creative people on the planet. If there is a need for organizing, event planning, gift baskets, decorations, or displays, she is the expert. She works in her areas of strength, and it frees me up to devote my time to life and business coaching, strategic thinking, and vision casting. Knowing your strengths allows you to stay in your sweet spot and stay energized. Over the long term, working from your strengths will prevent burn out. Donald O. Clifton and Paula Nelson's book *Soar with Your Strengths: A Simple Yet Revolutionary Philosophy of Business and Management*[6] taught me to differentiate between a strength and weakness. One of the questions to ask yourself is this: *What do I need to release to have more peace?* Falling in love with the journey is a daily choice, and one of the best tools for doing just that is a gratitude journal. Every morning, write down at least three things you are

What do I need to release to have more peace?

the most grateful for that happened to you within the past 24 hours. Maybe you didn't have a productive business day, and everyone said, "no." You can focus on the "no" you heard over and over, or you can choose to say, "I am thankful people were honest, and I now have more time to find people who are ready, willing, and able to partner with me today." Remember, you will get more of what you focus on, so this is a really big deal. One more thought on this before our exercise: Who would you rather work with, someone with an attitude of gratitude or someone who is always complaining about "If only…" or "What if…?"

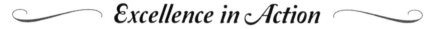

Excellence in Action

Write down the "If only…" thoughts that are keeping you from living fully in the present with an attitude of gratitude:

I would be happy if I only had:

I am so thankful for:

I would be fulfilled if I only had:

I am so thankful for:

I would be successful if I only had:

I am so thankful for:

Sometimes the answer to your "If only" or "What if" dilemma comes designed in a totally different package than you ever thought. I strongly believe that the opportunities you are most unwilling or afraid to try just might be the bridge to the life you were designed to live. The opportunity, this chance—perhaps it's the second or third chance—for change might seem bizarre, especially when those around you continue to affirm your fears and Pitiful labels. Yet, there is an audible whisper within: *What if this is it?*

- What if this is how you can enjoy work and spend more time with your family?

- What if this is your vehicle to have the platform you have always wanted to make a difference in the lives of others?

- What if this is your way to become financially independent without giving up your priorities or principles?

I remember when I asked myself that question 30 years ago when I started my business. Our daughter, Samantha, was only 18 months old, and I was active duty in the Air Force at the time. I designed and installed computer and telephone systems and worked rotating 12-hour shifts. My job required me to be on call around the clock and gone about ten days a month (to an undisclosed location). I was stationed at one Air Force base and my husband, Tom, was stationed at another. Plus I was taking college courses to wrap up my degree in electronic engineering. I was stressed out at work, and home wasn't any better.

We were dealing with massive amounts of physical and emotional stress along with maxed out credit cards. All this showed up in our daughter, Samantha. She clung to her babysitter (who watched her about 60 hours a week) and did not want to come home with me. That broke my heart. I wasn't a bad mom; I was just an exhausted mom. That is when I realized I had to make a change. I had invested seven years of my life in the Air Force and knew I could not be the wife and mom my family deserved if I chose to stay in that career field. So, I started my business, and today I have the privilege of serving as a Mary Kay Independent National Sales Director, the top position in the company. Tom and I have been happily married for 34 years, and Samantha and I are best friends because I chose to run a business from our home. Girlfriend, I wonder what fears are holding you back from your dream life?

Excellence in Action

Circle your greatest fear below or fill in with a fear not mentioned:

Fear of failure	Fear of success	Fear of making the wrong choice at the right time
Fear of rejection	Fear of approval	Fear of making the right choice at the wrong time

Now let's think about your worst case scenario and think through what could happen and how you would respond:

👠 What is my greatest fear?

👠 What is the worst thing that could happen if I did not succeed?

👠 How would I recover from that setback?

👠 What lessons could I learn from this experience?

How could I use this experience to coach others?

What would I have to give up in order to step into my dream life?

BE A BLESSING NOT A BURDEN

Now that you know you could survive your worst case scenarios, let's look at what could happen if you could make your dream life happen? Regardless of your situation, it is going to come down to you being a blessing in the lives of others instead of considering how others can be a blessing to you. This is service versus selling. You're going to lift others up instead of leaning on them. To do this, clarify your motive by asking yourself: *How I can be a blessing to this person?* instead of *What can this person do for me?*

The skills top salespeople use daily are the same skills that moms and ministry leaders use to move people from stuck to start and from failure to famous. Motive is the difference between "Using your business to grow your people instead of using people to grow your business." I was taught this concept at my first seminar by my mentor Arlene Lenarz, and I have built my entire business and ministry on this foundational concept. It's a great way to erase that Pitiful label of "I am not good at sales or coaching," and replace it with the Powerful label of "I am equipping those around me to be the best version of themselves."

By the way, did you know that coaching is selling? Anytime you are working with a group of people, and you are the one in charge of making sure an assignment gets completed, you are selling. You are selling them on themselves and their strengths; selling them on the benefits of growing out of their comfort zone; selling them on being inconvenienced to experience the sense of achievement for a job well done. Sometimes you will receive a tangible reward, like money or a prize, and sometimes your reward is intangible, like watching people grow into the very best version of themselves. Either way, it is a win-win scenario for everyone involved.

Remember that no matter how ill-equipped you feel, you can do this! I always laugh when I hear women say, "I can't sell" or "I can't lead." Nothing could be further from the truth because as wives and moms, we are selling all day long. You are selling your kids on the advantages of eating their vegetables or wearing their coat. When you lead a volunteer team, you are explaining the advantages of arriving 45 minutes early to plan and grow your ministry. If you are a business owner, you are extolling the virtues of creating a wow experience to your clients. Success happens when you offer a product or concept that adds value to others.

Make it a point to speak to others about how this opportunity is a blessing, and deliver what they are looking for with honesty and integrity. Over deliver and under promise your services. When I first started my business, I wanted to create a safe place for women to try a product or start a business. I made a personal commitment never to sell anything they did not need and to equip them with the information necessary to make an informed decision. I would do this by answering the *why* behind buying local. I decided to focus on how supporting a woman-owned business is good for local economies and how each purchase produces a positive national and global impact. I could do this without ever putting down another product or company. One of the best *why* lessons I've found is from Simon Sinek "Start with Why" on YouTube.[7] If you have been leading a group of people who are not buying into your vision or leadership, answering the basic *why* question first will get people on board quickly, and they will stick with you through the good and bad times. Your team wants to know *why* more than *what* or *how*.

A sure way to get off start and move forward is as simple as placing yourself in someone else's shoes and asking yourself how you can be a blessing to that person. You've probably heard that everyone is tuned into the radio station WIIFM (What's In It For Me?). I wonder how your life would be different if every morning you tuned out of WIIFM and tuned into WIIFT (What's In It For Them)? This small twist of the dial can make a huge difference in the peace and joy you experience every day, regardless of where you are on the scoreboard! The people you are working with recognize your "music" based on your radio station! Retune your station, and connect with your audience based on being a blessing and not a burden.

Now, I did not say it would be easy. What I have found is that motivating groups of people to move in the same direction is much like herding cats. Everyone is moving in all different directions and you are trying to get them to move in the same direction. However, when it gels together, and it always does if you don't quit, you can see God's thumbprint all over the process.

One of my favorite mantras is: It is all good because the whole story has not yet been written. Everything has to happen in a certain order for everyone involved to be blessed. We don't get to see the full picture until we are on the other side of the disappointment. When we look back, we will see we were protected from someone or something, that if it had all come together like we originally wanted, it would not have been this good. When you get frustrated with the timing or people, grab your can of glitter, and know that everything is falling into place—not falling apart.

Oh my! I get so excited to think about what you are going to do, so put this book down, take a deep breath, and make that call. It is time to accept that assignment, start that business, start that community group, volunteer somewhere, or do whatever that thing is that makes your heart beat faster and has the possibilities of a divine purpose. Take a few minutes and look back at your dream life list at the end of chapter 2. Write down a few steps you need to take to move toward achieving your dream life, and take action. Get off start! My sweet friend, be brave enough for you and all of those who are waiting on you to get out of that box and lead the way.

Excellence in Action

What is my next best step toward my dream life?

_____

_____

It's time to Erase and Replace whatever is holding you back from making that next best step:

PITIFUL	REPLACE	POWERFUL!
I don't know enough.		I will find the people with the answers.
I can't sell.		I will find a way to be a blessing.
I can't lead.		I will empower a team to partner with me.

Focus on the Solution, Not the Situation

Another way to get off start is to jump right in and start asking questions. This is a sure way to erase that Pitiful label "What if I don't have all of the answers?" or "I don't know if I'll be good enough." These thoughts occur to anyone starting something new: a new career, a new child, a new volunteer role, etc.

When hurricane Katrina came through Louisiana, I had the privilege of partnering with my church to set up one of the last shelters at the Hirsch Memorial Coliseum in Shreveport, Louisiana, for some of the final groups leaving New Orleans. The Red Cross was putting resources into other shelters at the time we opened up for our "guests," so we had very little guidance, just a lot of enthusiasm! I was handed a Post-it note that read: "Setup registration, transportation, and government assistance." I told Pastor Rick Berlin, "I can figure out the first two pretty easily, but I've never received government assistance. I don't know where to begin." He smiled his million-watt smile, "That is exactly why I picked you," he said. "You can talk to anyone. Just go out there and ask our guests what they are receiving, and we will set up as we go."

It was time to adjust my big-girl panties and get started. My heart was pounding as I approached the table where several people were talking. I asked permission to sit down then I explained why I was there, what we were doing, and how we needed their advice. The energy level went through the roof. We sat there for hours and collaborated on ideas concentrated on how to make life better in the short term for displaced Katrina survivors. When we discussed a subject I knew nothing about, someone would volunteer, "Wait, let me find...; they will know the answer." Before long, we were a group of 20 to 30 people who met daily to discuss what was and was not working effectively.

If we had waited until we had all the answers those people would not have had a place to sleep, food to eat, and we could not have started the process necessary to get them back home or relocated. We did not get it right all of the time, but we were honest with our guests, and they appreciated being part of the solution instead of the problem. They were our best source of information because they were empowered to help those around them. It was amazing to watch leaders rise up within that shelter. I have often wondered if that was the first time in many of their lives that anyone ever took the time to ask their advice, put it into action, and give them the credit? What a wonderful way to show a person their power to control their circumstances and help others.

Treating people with respect is one way to equip them to erase their Pitiful labels, replace them with the truth of a Powerful label, and encourage them to get out of their box! There is nothing, and I mean nothing, more rewarding than to watch this transformation happen before your very eyes. To watch someone's body language change, their shoulders pull back, their eyebrows rise, their voice grow stronger... My friend, when you can be the catalyst that equips others to remove that wedge of fear from their heads and hearts, that is where real life transformation begins. Without fail, when you reach out to help someone, your life is transformed in the process.

However, if you stay buried under the labels of fear, the people in your circle of influence will be stuck in that box because it was your hand that was supposed to lift them out of the box. Your words of truth and your belief that was supposed to help remove those limiting Pitiful labels from their life.

Those two weeks I spent serving displaced Katrina survivors at that shelter taught me more about getting off start and to just begin serving (even before systems are in place) than any other time in my life. I still remember when one of our guests came up to me with huge tears in her eyes. I don't know what she did for a living, but from our conversations I knew that she had lived a very hard life working on Bourbon Street. She shared she had never felt as loved and respected as she did while staying there in that shelter. I was blown away by her words. The shelter consisted of a thousand mattresses lying on a coliseum floor. This was the safest and most loved she had felt? I wondered how awful her life must have been that this was a highlight. I'm so glad we got off start before systems were in place. I'm so glad we got off start before we knew the next step. I'm so glad we showed the love of Christ before we shared the story of Christ.

I can still see the excitement of the 10-year-old boy who came running up yelling "Ms. Diana, we are getting a house with grass; no one in my family has ever had grass in their yard!" His Grandma rolled up in her wheelchair and gave me a hug and a thank you for helping get them connected with the right people. Lives and generations were changed by those who were brave enough to move out and start over. They did not know how to get off start either, but they knew that remaining the same was more terrifying than trying something new. They did not stay boxed in with "What if" and "If only." They took the opportunity to wedge their way through the fear of the unknown to recreate themselves. What most people don't realize is that this storm named Katrina allowed a second chance to many who would have never left New Orleans. An entire group of people are now out of the box designing a different life. What adventure is waiting on you?

Women of Excellence

AIR FORCE COMMAND CHIEF MASTER SERGEANT MARYANNE WALTS

Now, changing careers is not the "What if...?" answer for everyone, in fact, I went to Air Force Technical School with an amazing woman 36 years ago. We became best friends, got married the same year, had babies at the same time, and were both passionate about our careers. She decided to balance her military career and family, and does so in spectacular fashion. Maryanne Walts has proudly served in the Air Force and is now a Command Chief Master Sergeant. She and her husband, Jack, raised three amazing boys as she rose to the highest enlisted rank in the Air Force. Very few women have ever served in this position. She is making a difference in the lives of our troops every day by creating a healthy environment for them to serve our country. She is always looking for ways to improve their time in the military by showing them how to have a successful career without having to sacrifice their family on the way up the rank structure.

Our different choices highlight why it is so important not to follow the crowd and to make the best decision for you based on how you want to make your mark on the world. No one in her family had ever served in the military, and they could not understand why she chose a military career. Most of my family served in the military, and they could not understand why I embraced an entrepreneurial path. We both followed our passion and were both right in our choices. We are both so thankful we did not listen to people who loved us but wanted us to make the safe choice. We knew safe would never create excellence or excitement, and it would never provide the exhilaration of reaching the top of our career paths. Both Maryanne and I are very successful in all areas of our life, but we took different paths to get to the top. We both dealt with fears along the way and are both the first in our respective families to achieve this level of success. When we get together, we talk about the similarities in our career paths from the bottom to the top and how we never dreamed we would have the privilege to lead, impact, influence, and mentor this next generation all across the globe. I do it through my business, and she does it in the military. We have the same purpose and calling, just a different audience.

I wonder what audience is waiting on you to make a Be Brave decision and be true to your calling?

HOP INTO YOUR HOUSE SHOES; IT'S TIME TO CLEAR OUT THE CLUTTER IN YOUR MIND

I love winter and the holiday season. I love the smells, the family time, and I especially love hot cider. Don't you just love the smell and the warm, cozy feeling you get as it warms up your body? Once, just when I was feeling all warm and cozy and full of myself, I learned another lesson, and more labels were ripped away.

I was getting ready to speak at a small women's gathering when I took a drink of what looked and smelled like sweet cider. As it burned down my throat and I coughed up what felt like half my lung, I asked my sweet friend Jackie, "What did you put in your cider?"

"Honey, I haven't got any cider," she said in her slow southern drawl. As I tried to recover my breath, with mascara-stained tears running down my face, I very rudely said, "Jackie, what do you have in the slow cooker with the six matching cups on the counter?" She smiled and said as she laughed, "Why, Diana, that is potpourri!" Lesson learned. Things are not always as they appear. Now at speaking events, I drink bottled water only!

The conversations running around your head are not as they first appear either. To make a change, we need to slow down, be quiet, and take captive every thought to determine if it is Pitiful or Powerful. This is an ongoing Exercise in Excellence activity, and you are the only one who can do it. Make sure to monitor your thoughts every day, every hour, and sometimes, even minute by minute.

One of the most exciting results of monitoring your thoughts is realizing that changing the conversation in your head will change your legacy. Just take a second and let that sink in. Just think about the possibilities for you and for those who will follow in your footsteps. It is time to pull out another pair of shoes, so open up your mental closet and hop into your fun, fuzzy House Shoes. We are going to clean some house; clear out those cobwebs in your brain, and redecorate your mind and thoughts. We are going to choose to thrive on a daily basis, not just survive another day.

Let's start with something as simple as choosing to make a Be Brave decision. Most people choose one job or career or another; their choices are rooted in *either/or* thinking because choosing one thing over another is safe and easy, and it doesn't require much thought or creativity. But there is a life of *and* just waiting for you. The *and* life is one of abundance, the *either/or* life is one of scarcity. The *and* life is living in faith, while the *either/or* life is all about fear. Many of us are just one Be Brave moment away from stepping out of the box created by others and into a limitless life. You know that moment when you hold your breath and pull off the Band-Aid? It hurts for a second, but we know the quicker we remove it, the quicker we begin the healing process. A Be Brave moment can change the course of your life because you are choosing *and* over *either/or*.

Whenever a situation presents itself, find a way to combine both choices. If you want to be a doctor and work in ministry, do both. Become a doctor and donate a portion of your time to the underprivileged. So, you love working with teens and are called to run a business? Find a way to hire the kids as interns to enable you to mentor them in business.

You can do all things. You just can't do all things in all seasons. If you have small kids and work outside the home, then running the huge women's ministry might not be the best use of your time and energy right now. Why not consider working with a ministry tailored to your kids' age so you can stay involved in their lives? Baking 100 cupcakes is only wise for those who love to cook and have the time to spare. Maybe you can be like our daughter, Samantha. She is the paper-goods mom. Everyone knows they can count on Samantha to be at every event with lots of plates, napkins, and cups. This way, she doesn't miss time with Dakota or feel frustrated about those 100 cupcakes. She gets to be 100 percent in the moment with her friends instead of being distracted by a donut or to-do list.   If it doesn't bring you joy or create memories with those most important to you, don't do it. Let someone else shine in that role.

If people try to stop you from making that Be Brave choice to live in the world of *and*, just put on your Jesus Filter; pull out your can of glitter, and spray yourself. Bless their little hearts; they are doing the best they can! You could be the first person in your entire family tree who will think this new thought. You are blazing a new trail for others to follow. How exciting is that?

CHANGE YOUR THOUGHTS TO CHANGE YOUR LEGACY

Think about this thought process as a PowerPoint® presentation. When a situation arises, a slide appears in your mind. The slide contains an image that triggers a memory or emotion that can determine your reaction. An important element of living your dream life is to discover how you respond in various situations and change your response when necessary. For example: if you need to ask someone to volunteer for something at church or school, one of two slides will pop into your mind's eye.

The positive slide contains a picture of you presenting someone with a volunteer opportunity that will utilize their gifts and talents to partner with you as a team. That person will feel valued and appreciated because they were chosen from the group. Regardless of their response, this is a win-win conversation. You were able to speak truth into their life by acknowledging their gift set. Plus, you were able to remove an item from your to-do list, so you feel less stressed. Your Powerful label now becomes "I am a connector," "I can spot talent." "I help people find their sweet spot to serve."

The other slide is negative. This slide contains a picture of you presenting this same volunteer opportunity, only this time, your mind anticipates a "no" response. You feel rejected before you ever open your mouth. You imagine that you are a bother instead of a blessing. This is a lose-lose conversation. Because you are afraid of receiving a negative response, you don't ask them to partner with you, and the opportunity for that person to shine is lost. Plus, because you don't ask, you have more items on your to-do list. Now you're even more stressed.

In truth, if you don't ask, you can't know what the response will be. I believe motive comes into play when you are choosing slides. A selfless motive directs the spotlight on the other person. A selfish motive focuses on yourself. Just count the number of times you use either "I" or "me" in a conversation. That will tell you which motive you are operating in right then. When you choose this selfish slide, both parties are negatively impacted. She loses out on her chance to shine, and you are responsible for completing the project without support. This scenario confirms the "If it needs to get done, I must do it myself" mindset. This Pitiful label only causes exhaustion and unmet expectations. No one person can do it all. Empowering those around you to shine is a wonderful way to give back to others, so you can fully engage with those most important in your life.

Excellence in Action

Let's take a second to look at your to-do list and find at least one project you could give away to someone else.

Here are some suggestions:

- Housekeeping
- Child Care
- Tutoring for you and kids
- Lawn Service
- Beauty and Fashion Expert
- Financial Planner
- Business Coach
- Office/Computer Help
- Personal Chef
- Personal Trainer
- Spiritual Mentor

What would be the first project you would give away?

_____

_____

How would you feel without project this on your list? Did you know that when you delegate a task to someone else to complete, you also give up the emotional attachment? The best example I can give you is hiring a housekeeper. Granted, most of us can clean our houses better than anyone else, but we are trading our most precious commodity, which is our time, on something that does not grow our relationship with the Lord, our family, or key people in our business, ministry, or work. If you spent your entire morning cleaning your kitchen and your family accidentally spills something on the floor, you would be furious because they just wasted all of the time and energy you just put into that clean kitchen. See, you are emotionally attached to that task. Now, if you paid someone to clean your house and your family makes a mess, you can say, "Susie the housekeeper is going to be so mad at you all, you'd better wipe that up." You can always make more money to hire help, but you cannot make more time.

The most challenging part of this leadership lesson comes when you need more help, but you don't have available cash flow. This is why multiple streams of income are crucial for financial and emotional stability. I was always taught that you have to get the help before you can pay for the help. Then you have the time to invest in those activities that are designed to create relationships, growth, and income. Start out small, maybe consider bartering for housework. You might have a product or skill she needs, and the two of you can trade out services. There you see the win-win scenario at work again.

One more thought to get you out of your box. Did you know that one of the greatest privileges of creating wealth is creating financial opportunities for other people? You are investing in their dream lives by supporting their businesses. We have five to six virtual assistants who work with us at any given time, along with a housekeeper, lawn person, and a financial planner. The advantage of having access to money is the ability to partner with the best people in each area plus every time you pay them, you are investing in their dream life. You cannot find one person who can successfully fulfill all of these roles. Do what you do best, and let others use their strengths to shine.

Excellence in cAction

Let's keep stepping out of your box by filling in the lines below with the people you will empower with the projects you listed above. You might want to go back to the previous chapters to fill in the entire chart.

WHO CAN YOU EMPOWER? (CHAPTER 4)	PITIFUL LABELS (CHAPTER 2)	POWERFUL LABELS (CHAPTER 2)	DREAM LIFE (CHAPTER 1)
_____	_____	_____	_____
_____	_____	_____	_____
_____	_____	_____	_____
_____	_____	_____	_____
_____	_____	_____	_____

SELF-IDENTITY

Cut Out The Comparison Game

Another way to clear out the clutter in your mind is to stop playing the comparison game. The comparison game is dangerous because we compare our areas of weakness to the strengths of several people. We tend to create the perfect woman in our minds. She makes a million dollars a year, looks like a million, gives away millions, can speak to a million people as powerfully as she speaks to one. She is the one in a million to her family, and, to top it off, she is the one millions want to partner with in church and business. She is the Proverbs 31 woman times a million!

The problem with this image is that it is never just one woman who is all of these things, this is really six different women all rolled into one, and we are comparing "her" to the areas in our life where we feel weakest. No wonder it is so difficult to feel good about ourselves. Added to our game of self-comparison to this non-existent perfect woman, we face unrealistic images of women on television, in magazines, and on social media daily. It is amazing any of us ever leave the house. But none of that is reality. You cannot win this comparison game, so quit doing it. Focus on your strengths because they are the exact ones you need to fulfill your God-ordained purpose. You were uniquely designed, like a puzzle piece, to fit your purpose. You already have everything it takes. Uncover your strengths and use them! Sorry for the bunny trail. I don't know who needed that today, but there you go! Now back to getting more help.

I heard growing up, "Money doesn't buy happiness!" You know what I've learned? Only poor people say that, and it is not true.

Money can buy happiness because you get to choose who you live with, where you live, what you invest in, and the list goes on and on. With that being said, I don't believe money can buy joy. I personally believe joy comes with a personal relationship with Jesus Christ, not always trying to earn and re-earn your salvation or working to be good enough to get into heaven.[8] Joy is what you feel when you don't understand why things happen, but you know that God has your back. Joy is knowing the whole story is not yet written on this relationship or business opportunity because you are in a lesson-learning season. Now, depending on your religious beliefs, you may not agree with my definition of joy, and that is totally okay. Just know that happiness is circumstantial, and joy is a choice. Happiness is an outside job, and joy is an inside job.

There is nothing attractive about a woman buried by a to-do list she created but refuses to get help with. Make sure not to become one of those Hoover® vacuum people. These are the people in your life who suck all of the positive energy out of a room when they arrive. They are the type of people who make you feel like you have been sucked dry when you get off the phone with them. We all have those kinds of people in our lives. Let's just make sure we are not one of them.

Sometimes this type of control freak reaction is an indication of low self-esteem that displays itself as the Pitiful label, "I need to be all things to all people." If you lead most of your conversations with "I have so much to do," or "my list just keeps growing," or "I can't get any help; I have to do everything by myself," you might want to erase the "If I want it done right I have to do it myself" label. My friend, there is freedom in releasing this label and replacing it with "I will work in my gift zone and allow others around me to shine in theirs!" I suspect I will receive some thank you cards from your family when you do this Erase and Replace.

The decision to play a different slide is the bridge between being a person of mediocrity and a person of excellence. Achievement and happiness is not the result of pursuing perfection, it is the result of pursuing excellence. You don't have to be perfect to be successful or to live in excellence. Whew! Doesn't that eliminate a lot of pressure? Wow, that erases the "I have to be perfect and the best all the time" Pitiful label.

Keep in mind, as you are choosing different slides, that choosing the win-win slide will change your life and the way your kids see life too. Our daughter is one of the happiest and most positive people on the planet. I am so thankful I changed my thinking because she has grown up expecting only great and wonderful things. Last year, I left the dentist office with my mouth still a little numb, so my words were mumbled. I called Samantha to let her know about my new crown. She called me back, dancing around the room, shouting "Congratulations Mom, you earned another crown from the company. You are so deserving. I'm proud of you! How did you earn it?" We both had a good laugh when we sorted out the miscommunication. Oh my, I'm so thankful that she thinks of accomplishment and not pain when she hears the word crown.

What do your kids think first when presented with a situation that can be viewed as either positive or negative? I bet it looks a lot like yours. This is why it is important to change our thoughts. Thoughts do change our legacies!

THE SECOND CONVERSATION

I remember exactly where I was sitting when one of my mentors, Charlotte Kosena, taught the concept of the second conversation, and it totally changed the trajectory of my life. I sure hope it does the same for you. The second conversation is what happens in your thoughts immediately following a statement or situation. If I say to you, "Wow, you are such a talented leader," your next thought is your second conversation. You make a decision based on the way you perceive yourself whether to receive or reject the compliment. If your internal voice responds, *She's wrong*, or *I don't believe that*, or *Somebody like me could never lead because I am unworthy*, you affirm your Pitiful labels and reject the Powerful label I am attempting to give you. Each time someone says something positive about you, this negative internal conversation will occur.

Sometimes, when you are on a track that is so far beyond anything you could ever hope for or imagine, your second conversation unconsciously puts a lid on your success, and you stay in the box! Let's hop into our House Shoes. We must clean out these crazy cobwebs of confusion.

My background wired me to be afraid of abundant success, and as I grew my business, this label created struggle for me. Each time I neared a breakthrough, I would self-sabotage to prevent myself from reaching my goal. Unconsciously, I would create chaos within my inner circle that required my attention which would distract my attention from performing the necessary activity to move ahead professionally.

I spent years attempting to earn the top performers trip because I did not think Tom and I were "those kind of people." Each time I was included in a conversation about those fancy parties, all I could think—my second conversation—was how different those exotic trips were from my everyday lifestyle. When we threw a party, we just put beer in the fridge and watched what happened. In my thoughts we didn't belong at those fancy dinners. Perfect etiquette is not the primary mealtime objective in my family. Our typical table setting is pretty simple, a fork and knife. If you want a biscuit, we just throw you one across the table. But at these fancy dinners, there is a whole arsenal of silverware and not a biscuit to be seen!

This particular trip was an Alaskan Cruise. Tom said to me, "Baby, whatever you need to get fixed in your head and business, please get it fixed, so we can go on this trip!" Yikes! I had to make some changes. My mantra became "No excuses, no drama, no fear, no tears." I put up goal posters (see graphic) and vision boards all over my house. (A vision board is a collage of pictures that represent the life you want to live, houses, trips, donations, etc.) I recorded my positive affirmation and listened to that every morning and every night. (A positive affirmation is you visualizing

yourself having achieved your goal and looking back at your success as if it is already fact.) I changed my voicemail message and then began to introduce myself as the Future Trip Sales Director Diana Sumpter. Then, slowly, my business started to grow. Remember earlier we talked about how the subconscious goes to work to create whatever we say we want? Well, it was happening! Who would have ever thought that a recording and poster boards all over my house could make that much difference, but they really did. I had been teaching people about goal posters and positive affirmation for years, but I thought I was past all of that silly stuff.

What happened along the way was that my mind pivoted from "we don't belong" to "we are going to get this done because my man wants to go to Alaska." By rewiring my input, I changed the outcome. I did not work harder or learn any new skills. I simply did what I loved to do with a different perspective and purpose. On the last day of the year, everything started to fall apart—everything except my vision of standing at the airport with our tickets. I could see what we were wearing and our luggage at the check-in counter. The vision was crystal clear. By the end of the day, we qualified for the trip because we focused on helping others reach their goals and did not give up. Those posters and affirmations do work. You might want to grab a Sharpie® and start one right now.

On the first night of the cruise, it was finally time to erase that "We don't belong" Pitiful label. I remember thinking we needed to order room service before we went because the servings were small, and we loved to eat! My friend promised me there would be plenty of food, so we showed up really hungry. After a crazy looking salad and bread that stood up in a vase, they brought out these incredible hand-carved ice swans with what appeared to be ice cream in the middle. I leaned over to her and said: "I told you I should have ordered room service. They are already serving dessert, and there was no meat!" Come to find out, the sorbet was to clean my palette (I did not know I had one), so I could enjoy the other five courses that were on the way.

Do you see? Things are not always as they appear. If fear of the unknown doesn't trick you into you leaving the table, you will have the opportunity to enjoy the entire experience. More is coming. As it turns out, knowing which of the different forks to use with each course has nothing to do with being successful; it is traits like integrity, honesty, and a strong work ethic that make the real difference on whether you belong at the head table. It is crucial to our legacy to know that we are enough, enough to sit at banquet seat of life and not just eat the crumbs on the floor!

Excellence in Action

What second conversations in your mind are holding you back from your dream life? Once you recognize those Pitiful labels, go ahead and do an Erase and Replace:

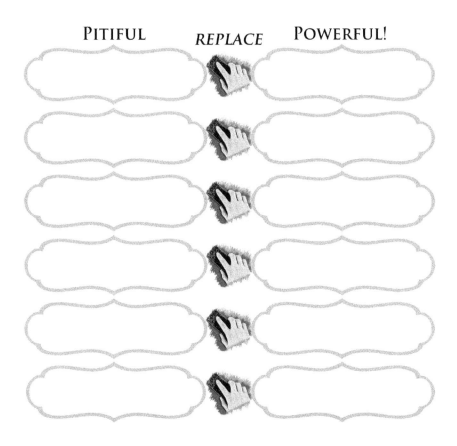

PITIFUL   *REPLACE*   POWERFUL!

Women of Excellence

SUSAN REEVES

(Shared by her daughter Weslee Schroeder)

"Never let anyone tell you what that baby can or can't do!" These words were spoken to Susan Reeves's momma after polio struck her healthy baby's 13-month-old body, leaving her unable to walk or stand without braces and crutches. Those words became a war cry for Susan her entire life. She carried herself in a way that most people completely forgot that her legs didn't work. She snow skied, jumped rope, carried her lunch tray, played tag, and rode pigs just like every other country kid. She believed she could, so she did. Having polio did not slow Susan down or diminish her life choices. She went on to marry the love of her life for almost 40 years, have three children, five grandchildren, work a full time job, and volunteer at church.

At 60, she was diagnosed with breast cancer and underwent a double mastectomy followed by months of chemotherapy. Six weeks after being deemed cancer free, Susan was diagnosed with leukemia. The next months and years were some of the hardest, most physically trying of her life. When most would have asked "why me?" she got up every day, put her makeup on, and readied herself to fight.

Susan used her story to lift up others who found themselves in similar situations. She had a list of women she sent personal texts of encouragement to every morning, offering them first-hand wisdom and strength only someone who has been there could provide. Watching her battle cancer with an already crippled body was empowering as she defied the odds until her death in April of 2017. Susan's legacy is one that reminds us that we get to decide how we react to what life throws at us and to never let anyone tell us what we can or can't do!

COMMANDEER YOUR COMBAT BOOTS; IT'S TIME TO CHARGE INTO THE BATTLE FOR YOUR THOUGHTS

S hooting is one of my favorite hobbies. I like to use all types of guns: small, large, automatic weapons… You name it, and I love to shoot it. I grew up on a small farm in a military family, so shooting was something we did for fun. When I joined the Air Force, I qualified as an expert marksman using both an M-16 rifle and a .38 caliber handgun. When our family gets together for the holidays, someone always gets a new rifle, gun, or crossbow, and we head down to our meadow for target practice. Normally, I shoot as good as—or sometimes better than—the guys in our family (and they are all military or ex-police), so I got the nickname Dynamite

Di. Tom has called me that for years, and I think it is a cute name for this sassy shooting southern gal.

Last year, we hauled all the guns and ammunition down to the meadow and set everything up. I lined up the target and started firing, but something didn't seem right. Tom hollered, "What's up, Dynamite? You are missing everything!" *This just can't be*, I thought. I put my head down on the gun barrel and fired again. Again, shots went everywhere except where I wanted them. Then it dawned on me that after my fiftieth birthday, I had started having trouble seeing both close up and far away. I have contacts to correct each problem: one set for long distance and one for short. The problem was that I was looking through my short-distance contacts. I started laughing because no matter how hard I tried, I couldn't even see the end of the rifle! No more Dynamite Di here. I now have to wear my glasses to hit the target because I can't hit what I do not see.

Isn't that true in life? There was a time the target—your dream life—was crystal clear and your eyesight was perfect. Then, life started to happen, and your vision blurred a little at a time. The change was so slow and slight that you did not even notice. Then, before you knew it, you could not even see the target, and you couldn't remember what your sight was set on in the beginning.

Without focus, your target will continue to get more and more blurry until one day you will just quit trying. The target is still there, but someone else will step up to complete the task because the need didn't go away. You just have not done your part. Think about Queen Esther in the Bible. Her Uncle Mordecai told her that if she kept quiet, deliverance for the Jews would come from someone else, and she and her family would perish. He also said that she might have come to her royal position "for such a time as this" (Esther 4:14, NIV).[9] Girlfriend, this blessing, this God-ordained purpose called your dream life, is yours for the taking. It was laid on your heart. It is your responsibility to finish what you started. Clear your vision and take aim. Choose to be courageous and commandeer your Combat Boots! It is time to go into a daily battle for your thoughts.

Your life will reflect your most dominant thought. Sometimes it is a daily battle to keep that thought positive and focused on your goals. Think about your life as a scale, one side is positive and the other is negative. Every day will have both positive and negative experiences; you decide which side receives your attention. The experiences you choose to focus on will determine what you attract because what you focus on will grow. This can be good or bad, depending on what you are focused on accomplishing. Focusing on negative perfectionist thoughts or thoughts of perceived setbacks will impact your words. Your words will impact your energy, and your energy will impact your attraction factor. On the other side, good positive energy attracts good energetic people and possibilities your way.

If you don't believe it, for just one day force yourself to speak out loud uplifting things about the people and situations in your life. You will feel the difference in your energy, and you will notice a different response from others right away. Can you imagine a week of this type of change? How about a lifetime of choosing to focus on the positive?

You can tip the scale based on what you are putting in your mind. Here is my favorite story about the power of focus; it is a clear reminder that even if we can't see the finish line, it is still waiting for us!

FLORENCE CHADWICK: WHAT ARE YOU FOCUSING ON?

In 1952, Florence attempted to swim the 26 miles between Catalina Island and the California coastline. As she began, she was flanked by small boats that watched for sharks and were prepared to help her if she got hurt or grew tired.

After about 15 hours, a thick fog set in. Florence began to doubt her ability, and she told her mother, who was in one of the boats, that she did not think she could make it. She swam for another hour before asking to be pulled out, unable to see the coastline due to the fog. As Florence sat in the boat, she found out she had stopped swimming just one mile away from her destination.

Brian Cavanaugh, in *A Fresh Packet of Sower's Seeds*, noted that Florence told a reporter, "Look, I'm not excusing myself, but if I could have seen land, I know I could have made it." The fog had made her unable to see her goal, and it had felt to her like she was getting nowhere.

Two months later, Florence tried again. The fog was just as dense, but this time she made it. After 13 hours, 47 minutes, and 55 seconds, she reached the California shore; breaking a 27-year-old record by more than two hours and becoming the first woman ever to complete the swim.

Florence said that she kept a mental image of the shoreline in her mind while she swam. She later swam the Catalina channel on two additional occasions.[10]

YOUR INNER CIRCLE

Another way to tip the scale toward positive is to spend more time with positive people, and do your best to avoid the negative ones. The five adults we spend the most time with determine who we become because they continuously pour into our lives, good or bad. We know this is true with our kids; we preach it all of the time. I wonder when we stopped applying it to ourselves?

Excellence in Action

Make a list of the five adults you spend the majority of your time with on a daily basis.

1. Put a + (addition) sign by their name if after being with them you feel better about yourself and your future.

2. Put a − (subtraction) sign by their name if you feel depressed, discouraged, and downright defeated when they leave.

3. Put an = (equal) sign if you don't feel any better or any worse.

1. _____ ____

2. _____ ____

3. _____ ____

4. _____ ____

5. _____ ____

If you have more +'s (addition signs) then you have a hopeful, future-focused outlook on life, regardless of your circumstances or position on the scoreboard.

If you have more ='s (equal signs) then you are up and down like a roller coaster, depending on your circumstances and your time of the month!

If you have more −'s (negative signs) you are frazzled and frustrated with life regardless of the circumstances or position on the scoreboard.

Let's avoid those subtraction people at all costs. Commandeer your Combat Boots and march right out the door when they come around to complain. Deposit more weight on the positive side of your scale by controlling who is pouring into your hopes and dreams.

It is time to change your inner circle, media input, and attitude to begin attracting positive results in all areas of your life. So, you don't believe me? I issue you a 21-day challenge to avoid the people who subtract or add nothing to your life. Instead, invest your time with those who add to your life. Here is a quote from an unknown person that defines a real friend, one that you would draw a big plus sign by their name: "A friend is someone who knows the song in your heart and can sing it back to you when you have forgotten the words."

After 21 days of investing time with the people who add to your life, reach out to me and let me know the difference in your outlook and attitude!

After I put this scale mentality in place and changed who I allowed in my inner circle, I started to soar up the career ladder. I started to believe that we did belong with the top achievers. Then out of nowhere, those crazy labels from my past started to again dominate my thoughts. Poverty mentality labels like "rich people are bad" and "they are never happy" began playing in my thoughts. It didn't stop with those two labels either. "Rich people use people" was another one. "They always lose their family on the way to the top." On and on it went. These thoughts combined with my fundamental evangelical upbringing that taught rich people can't go to heaven really put me in a conundrum. I could be successful, but no one would like me. I wouldn't fit in; I would lose my friends and family and was going to hell all because I was rich and successful. Wow! That made it hard to motivate myself to work.

Little by little, I uncovered the lies by listening to my second conversation. Then I replaced my Pitiful labels with Powerful labels and built a very successful career without losing my faith, family, or friends. Tom and I have been happily married for 35 years and gone on 17 of those world-class company trips. We even had the privilege to travel and teach in both Prague and Oxford! Who would have ever thought such a life was waiting outside that crazy box?

Our daughter Samantha has become one of the first women on our side of the family to graduate from college. She is secure in who she is as a woman and mom. Samantha and I have very different personality styles, so it took a lot of courage on her part to be who God intended her to be and not a mini-me.

I am actively involved in my church, volunteer when I choose, and can invest when felt led to support a cause or mission. I have been able to care for aging parents, still enjoy time with my sister and her children, and I go shopping with my girlfriends anytime I want. I only share this because I want you to have more evidence that you can create abundant success and healthy relationships at the same time.

Your dream life will look different from mine. In fact, it will probably look different than any life you have seen. Because of your unique design, your DNA, your passions, and your purpose you will desire different priorities in your life. When you are true to who you are called to be, your dream life will look just like YOU. You just need to make a few adjustments to your head, heart, and habits to make this happen. It is closer than you think.

HEALTHY HABITS

Here are a few daily habit adjustments you can make to align your head, heart, and habits.

THE FIRST AND LAST 30

The first and last thirty minutes of each day are precious. Use them wisely. Here are three quick activities to do each morning.

- **Stop using your cell phone as your morning alarm clock.** (Don't even bring it into the bedroom.) By eliminating the cell phone, you won't be bombarded with texts, emails, and social media alerts the first 30 minutes of your morning.

- **Use a gratitude journal.** Write down a list of positive things that happened the day before to remind yourself of the good in your life. This list can contain a personal breakthrough in thinking or a relationship. It can be something business related, or even something as small as a sense of peace that you can't describe. When you start your day like this instead of being assaulted with all of those emails, texts, and social media messages, you build your reserves to take on the day. If you haven't started already, there is a gratitude journal starting on page 159 of this book.

- **10 minutes of positive input.** Start reading 10 pages of a positive book to align your heart and head for the day, or while you're getting dressed, listen to a positive message for 10 minutes.

The last 30 minutes are equally important. Add these habits to your right-before-bed routine.

👠 **Build your Six Most Important List.** This list contains the six most important things you need to accomplish the next day. You will want to make up this list at the end of each day, before you leave your office or when you put the kids down to bed. Over and over, Mary Kay Ash taught about the Six Most Important list. The idea actually belongs to Ivy Lee, an efficiency expert who once called on Charles Schwab when he was president of Bethlehem Steel.[11] You might be thinking, *Girl, I have 60 things on my list every day!* That is exactly why you feel defeated every day. You rarely achieve a sense of accomplishment, and you lack the time to do the important things in life. So trust me on this, just write down the six most important things, not the 60 that need to be done!

👠 At night, before you go to bed, change out what you read or watch. What you end your day with affects your dreams and energy throughout the night. This was an area that Tom and I used to argue about. He loved watching the "Walking Dead™" on Sunday nights, and I kept telling him we needed to stop. "We can't watch that before we go to bed! How are we going to have a miracle-filled Monday if the last thing we heard the night before going to sleep was zombies being bludgeoned to death?" We decided to compromise. He would watch it another night, and we would watch something together on the sports or animal channel. The change made a positive difference for both of us. He even commented (a little sarcastically), "Can't have a magnificent Monday if we watch this!"

🔻 Right before you go to sleep, take a few minutes to review your day. Look for the blessings, say your positive affirmation, and visualize your next goal becoming a reality.

PLAN A PEACEFUL, PURPOSEFUL WEEK

At the beginning of each week, make a list of everything you need to do that week in your home, business, and church. This is called a mind dump. Write down everything that needs to happen during the week along with things that bug you around the house or in your business. Then, create an extermination list for those bugs. Highlight the activities that only you can do, and spread them out during the week. The other to-do items, delegate to others. By partnering with others to check off the items on your list, they have the opportunity to shine in their gift set.

There is another big difference in those who are at the top of their game and still have a great faith and family life and those stuck in the middle or at the bottom. It is where and how they invest their time and money. I hear women all the time complain about their busy schedules, but they have no idea what they need to change in order for them to have a peaceful, productive week. Top performers can quickly provide a clear description of their most productive day, week, month, and year. They know their target (what they are shooting at). It doesn't mean they always hit it, but they get a whole lot closer because they know what it takes to be successful in all areas of their lives.

Excellence in Action

1. Make a list of everything that needs to be done this week on a separate sheet of paper. Put a star by the action items that only you can do, like your quiet time, exercise, time with your man, kids, etc.

2. Now let's take a minute to build your perfect week, assuming everyone did what they said they would do, and no one got sick or postponed appointments. This is what you are striving for each week—your target.

	Sunday	Monday	Tuesday	Wednesday	Thursday	Friday	Saturday
5:00 AM							
6:00 AM							
7:00 AM							
8:00 AM							
9:00 AM							
10:00 AM							
11:00 AM							
12:00 PM							
1:00 PM							
2:00 PM							
3:00 PM							
4:00 PM							
5:00 PM							
6:00 PM							
7:00 PM							
8:00 PM							
9:00 PM							
10:00PM							

Each Sunday, fill in a new plan sheet. Try to plan each week to achieve your dream week. As you go along, look for tasks to delegate. Your loved ones will appreciate the added time with you. One of my favorite quotes is from the funeral of my friend Barbara Johnson. Her son-in-law challenged us all to "Live a life that when people think of you, they thank the Lord for you!" What a way to be remembered.

Focus on Financial Security

Now that we have looked at how to manage your time, let's look at how to manage your money! I have been taught to tithe 10 percent to my local church, save for emergencies ($2,000 in cash), have four to six months of income put away, and to invest in a retirement plan. If you want to work with a pure motive, you have to get a handle on your finances. Here are a few statistics for you to consider from Statistical Brain Drain.[12]

- 52% of women are expected to work past retirement age.
- 54% of women have no money left after paying bills.
- 35% of single women have a retirement account.
- 87% of impoverished elderly are women.

Here are a few more statistics to show how fragile our finances are in the US.

- The average American woman earns $37,000 each year.[13]
- One-third of Americans report they have no retirement savings.[14]

- The average American household with student debt owes about $49,000. Graduates in their 20s spend more than $350 each month on average student loan payments and interest.[15]

- There is currently 1.31 trillion in student loan debt with a delinquency rate of 11.2 percent.[16]

- Average US credit card debt has balances totaling $16,883.[17]

This is a wake-up call for all of us! Compare your financial situation with these numbers to evaluate your financial health. "Let's analyze ourselves and not criticize ourselves," as my friend, Crystal Gardner shares during her coaching sessions. Let's look at how you can create multiple streams of income, so you do not have to rely on only one source.

Without multiple income streams, you will reach a crossroad in life that forces you to choose finances over faith and family. Your job pays you once for what your position is worth, not what you are worth. And they will replace you when they find someone to work cheaper. Having a single source of income is dangerous because you are trading your time for money. You have a limited number of hours to work, and you have to show up to get a paycheck. Showing up requires everyone in your household, including yourself, to remain healthy.

This past year, my dad came to live with us. He arrived with an advanced case of Alzheimer's. He had experienced slight symptoms for years, and my sister Donna took amazing care of him. As the years went on, we noticed his symptoms were getting worse but ignored the signs. We did not want to acknowledge that we were losing Dad. A surgery Donna had to undergo combined with an official Alzheimer's diagnosis forced us to make hard decisions. Donna could not keep Dad at his home, so we decided he would come to live with Tom and me. I always promised Dad we would take care of him if he needed a place to live out his final years. That is one reason I worked so hard to create the income needed to purchase a home large enough for all of us.

I remember going to the neurologist and her hearing her say, "Diana, you cannot keep your dad at home. He is too far gone; he doesn't even know who you are. You obviously have a successful career, so you cannot provide the around the clock observation he needs."

It was a relief that I could tell her that I work from home, my husband is retired military and works with me, and someone is home all the time. I also let her know that I set my hours and have income coming in whether I show up to work or not. Dad was coming home with me. I know she did not believe me, but I knew I had built a successful business during the good times, and I now had a business that would take care of us during the challenging times. In fact, during the time that Dad stayed with us, I experienced my biggest year ever. When he passed away (less than a year after he arrived), I was so thankful he spent his last year with either me or Donna. He was always with family. I was so thankful that neither of us ever had to focus our time on making a living instead of investing our time making a comfortable life for Dad.

I share this story to show you the power of creating multiple streams of income. A second job can make a huge difference in your financial security. There are a lot of options right now, in fact, Intuit did a survey and predicted that by the year 2020, 40 percent of Americans will be independent contractors.[18] Some of the major advantages of independent contracting over employee status is the flexibility and career path advancement on your own terms. You can live out your dream life with your priorities in order because you are the boss. If you are looking at adding in additional streams of income in this economy we live in, you will need to do your research.

Here are a few questions you might want to ask before starting something new:

- What is the driving force behind the culture and legacy of this company?

- Where does the company invest their charitable dollars?

- What kind of education and ongoing mentorship is available?

- Is there a retirement option?

- Is there a buyback for inventory or guarantee for client purchases?

- Is this company part of a protection agency or association?

- Are there multiple streams of income and bonuses available?

- Do they have a consumable product?

You will need to find a company that you are proud to represent, aligns with your value system, and provides you the opportunity to showcase your talents. Whether your talent and passion is interior design (because you love to decorate), child care (because you love kids), direct sales (because you love to share a product or coach and mentor), a pet-sitting service (because you love animals), or anything else that brings you joy. One the best quotes I have ever heard is from Mark Twain: "Find a job you enjoy doing, and you will never have to work a day in your life."[19]

When creating multiple streams of income, you can pay off debt, build savings, invest in retirement funds, and have money left over to invest in people and projects that are important to you. It is such a privilege to be able to create abundant wealth because you have more money to donate to those who do not have the opportunity to generate income. There are many places around the world where that is not an option, especially for women. I hear people say, "I don't need much money." That is a self-centered Pitiful label. An others-centered Powerful label is "I want to create as much wealth as possible, so I can invest in other people's dreams." Imagine your life as one where your driving force is getting to decide which charities to support instead of deciding which bill you have to pay. Girlfriend, we have to get you out of that box quickly, charities and causes are waiting for you to write that check!

 *Excellence in Action*

Let's put together a money plan:

-  To what charities or churches will you be donating your tithe?

- What is your next best step to building your cash savings?

- What is your next best step to building three months of salary?

- What is your next best step to building your retirement fund?

- How can you create more streams of income?

The next thing top performers invest in is professional and personal growth. If you have to decide to give something up, give up a trip to the store or that new outfit, so you can afford to attend a conference with the top people in your industry. Change out that lunch with the people who whine, complain, and gossip for a networking event where you can make new connections and learn a new skill. Invest your time listening to positive speakers while you are driving to work, working out, or getting ready for the day instead of music that does not have a powerful message of hope. Just think about the new crease you are putting in your brain with all of the new thoughts, and even better, if you have kids in the car, you are setting them up with powerful thoughts from the beginning.

See your day as you want it to be. If it is foggy, commandeer those Combat Boots to battle for your thoughts! Are you are visualizing your day as either Powerful or Pitiful? You get to decide. Did you know that visualization is another powerful tool used by top performers in every field? Athletes run their performance in their heads before they are in the spotlight. Olympic divers stand outside the pool with their eyes shut as they twist their bodies through each step. In their minds, they have scored a perfect 10 dive before they ever touch the ladder.

I challenge you to visualize your day and your next victory every morning. Put a picture on your mirror as a reminder. Trash your house with vision boards and goal posters. Most people will think you are crazy and that doing those things are silly, but those are the broke, beaten-down people in your life. They might even make fun of you and try to pull you off focus. Grab your can of glitter and ignore them. Instead, surround yourself with those brave, bold people in your life who will get excited about your renewed passion! These are the people who will help you find more quotes and pictures to remind you of where you are going. They are your greatest cheerleaders and prayer partners. For the last 40 years, my mentor, Karen Piro, has been sharing, "If you would not trade places with a person, don't take advice from them."

My sweet friend, it is time to win that daily war of words in your head. It is time to pull out the big guns to blast your way out of that silly box. It is time to come face to face with the real enemy, the woman you see every day in the mirror. You are the only one who can choose your life, and it is hidden in your daily routine and the door you step through every day. I have done a little recon mission to uncover the secret path to the Land of Excellence. Are you ready to join the other Women of Excellence? Keep going, you are closer than you think!

Women of Excellence

JEA GACKOWSKI

My friend Jea, has more degrees than an oven and a resume as long as your arm. She is the "fixer" in her family and at work. If there is a problem, Jea is your girl. I asked her how she got this label and how long it impacted her life choices. Jea shared that she was driven by two thoughts growing up. The first thought was she felt like she was not good enough because she grew up without a lot of money, so she decided to do whatever it took not to find herself on that side of scarcity again. The second thought was to take care of everything for everyone. When Jea was a little girl, she was told her mom became very sick because of exhaustion. That statement rocked her to the core. She made the commitment no one in her life would ever become sick again from exhaustion because she would take care of everything.

Because of these two Pitiful labels: "I'm not good enough" and "I will take care of everything," she lived a very unfulfilling life, trading career over children and finances over friends. Finally she realized that her life was not supposed to be wrapped around these labels. She made a big career change and went from employee to entrepreneur. She then focused on living by the true Golden Rule, treating others as she wants to be treated; not by the corporate Golden Rule, he who has the gold rules. She no longer has to prove herself to the board of directors because she is the one who directs her business. Many lives have been impacted because of her Be Brave choice to step out of that corporate box to enjoy the freedom of owning her own business. There are storm survivors who received tractor-trailer loads of food and supplies, local businesses being promoted through networking events, and local domestic violence shelters getting grants. This is the power of changing your labels. Change the label to change the focus; change your focus to change your future.

TIE UP YOUR TENNIS SHOES; IT'S TIME TO RUN OUT OF THE LAND OF THE LAZY

D o you have a favorite song that just makes your heart pump faster? One that, when it comes on, gets you so excited that you feel powerful beyond words? I believe that a song can get you through the times in your life when your goals seem out-of-reach, and it appears there is no way things could come together.

Have you ever heard the song "Ancient of Days" performed by Ron Kenoly?[20] It's a good one, my friend. The lyrics and music are so powerful that it's easy to lose yourself in the moment! That is exactly what I did. I remember the moment as if it were yesterday. I was driving down I-49 from Shreveport down to Natchitoches to speak at an event. We were working on reaching a huge goal. (You know the kind, a barf bag goal; one that makes you want to throw up every time you think about it.) The end of the month was closing in quickly, and I had no idea how we were going to wrap up our goals. Deep down, though, I knew it would happen. I just needed to stay in motion, keep a super positive attitude, and expect success.

As I drove down the road, the negative thoughts and fears began to overtake my thoughts, and I could feel myself losing the battle. I did the only thing I knew to do: pray and put on some seriously strong praise and worship music. (Sometimes I prefer a little Van Halen or AC/DC, but that was not what I needed that day!) "Ancient of Days" kicked in, and I cranked up the speakers as loud as they would go. I started singing at the top of my lungs with my hand raised high in praise to the Lord. (I did keep one hand on the wheel.) Thankfully, I was alone because my gift set does not include one ounce of singing, humming, or anything to do with music ability—only unbridled enthusiasm.

This trip was one I had made a hundred times before, and I knew the speed limit dropped to 55 mph, but I was so caught up in the song and visualizing my dream that I missed that little ole' speed-limit sign! My spiritual praise and hopeful expectation were interrupted by blue lights in my rearview mirror. Immediately, I pulled over. I already knew my mistake, opened my door, and said to the sweet young police officer, "I am so sorry I was speeding, but I was just praising the Lord. You must listen to this song; it will change your whole day!" Then, I turned the volume all the way up for him for him to enjoy. He stared at me like I had three heads, and I realized I needed to take it down a notch, or I would be starting my prison ministry before the day's end.

I turned down the music, smiled, and confessed, "I totally deserve a ticket; I am really sorry." The young man started to smile and said, "Ma'am there is no way I could look my grandma in the eye if I gave you a ticket for praising the Lord too much. However, I do need you to slow down, so you don't go see Him today!"

There is nothing like the power of passion. Nothing is more powerful, more contagious, or more engaging than a person passionately pursuing a vision. It keeps you up at night, wakes you up early, and makes you brave and courageous! So why are we all not out there tying up our Tennis Shoes and chasing down our dreams?

THREE DOORS

We must choose Powerful over Pitiful every day regardless of our circumstances. Every morning we are presented with three doors, Door #1, Door #2, and Door #3, and we live in the land that lies behind the door we choose. Just like the Let's Make a Deal™ television show, you either get the gag gift or a brand new car! The difference between the show and your life is that your choices impact the lives of others. The door you choose most often is the one constructing your legacy. The life you are living right now is the result of a series of daily choices.

Take a deep breath and let us only peek into the Land of the Lazy. We don't want to go all the way in and linger there with those lazy folks. I can talk about them because they are too lazy to read a book like this or even make it this far. So pat yourself on the back for making it further than the masses. We are going to talk about what lies behind this door because we don't want to lounge around in there for an extended amount of time. What is behind this door? Look out! There are Pitiful, contagious labels flying all over the place and no one living here wants to get rid of them.

The Land of the Lazy is a world filled with guilt, frustration, doubt, and discouragement. Picture a ship on the sea being thrown around, tossing and turning, and never going anywhere. The Land of the Lazy is filled with people who are mastered by their emotions; there is no purpose to their life. Creative avoidance runs rampant through this place. No one is doing what needs to be done when it needs to get done. You hear a lot of "I will do that after I wash the dishes," or "I will do that when I am married or have kids." The avoidance excuses go on and on. Their motto is "It can't be done because we have lint in our belly button." It doesn't take much to distract, dissuade, or discourage this group of underachievers.

They spend their days just waiting to get in the mood to do something. "Imma Gonna" is Queen Bee here. You know her, "Imma gonna do this" and "Imma gonna do that." Another name for this place is Someday Isle. Someday, I'll start that business. Someday, I'll start saving. Someday, I'll really make a difference. Someday, however, is not a day of the week, so change never happens!

People who live in the Land of the Lazy are interested in making an impact in their world but only when it is exciting. They start out strong but quickly stall out. They are not committed to finishing strong. You can tell they are not committed because when things get complicated or uncomfortable, they quit. When rejections start rolling in, and the daily grind becomes boring, they start looking elsewhere for their next excitement fix. They are blame-game masters. They blame their past, their family, their boss, their coach, the government, or even the weather. These are the people who never look in the mirror and take responsibility for their daily choices, their attitude, or work ethic. Their lives are engulfed in crisis, chaos, and confusion.

POND OF PROCRASTINATION

In the center of the Land of the Lazy is the Pond of Procrastination, and this pond feeds into every relationship and choice that happens here. Peace does not live behind Door #1. Keep in mind that procrastination is the strongest poison to a peaceful life. Those who live here don't take care of the right things at the right time. They spend their time freaking out because their timing is off. They are late on that project. The car is out of gas, and their debit card is at the house! They never have time for the important people in their lives because they are always playing catch up or clean up. There are no healthy relationships here because they are always on the phone or checking their social media.

Procrastination is the strongest poison to a peaceful life.

As you look around more closely, you see a lot of fear in action, not faith in action. The

residents here are too busy catching up on yesterday's work to fit morning quiet time into their schedules. They have to clean up their finances because they did not tithe or save first—or they bought more things hoping to make themselves feel more important. You can see their exhaustion. These folks are living a life someone else chose for them. They never change careers, commit to that relationship, or start that business. They remain the same year after year because if nothing changes, nothing changes.

Does any of this sound familiar? I know it does to me because I have wrestled with these same types of choices and had to pay the price for my laziness. There are few things worse than getting lulled into this Land of the Lazy little by little, watching the days go by, and just waiting for the perfect time to start living the life you once dreamed of.

Have you ever felt yourself drowning in the Pond of Procrastination? Isn't it funny how we can be disciplined in one area and undisciplined in others? I believe the common denominator is: When passion and purpose are present, discipline is never a problem.

When passion and purpose are present, discipline is never a problem.

Have you ever had a day with an ongoing mind battle about where to invest your time? You thought about what needed to be done all day long, but at the end of the day, you realized you had been defeated again. You were busy all day, but not busy doing the things that bring you closer to your dream life. That is exactly where I have been with this book and my blog.

I started writing this book more than three years ago. In the beginning, I did well. I created a writing schedule and kept to it. But slowly, daily writing slipped off my radar. I used a million excuses not to write. The real reason I couldn't write is that my *why*, my purpose for writing this book, was not clear. So, putting off the task was easy.

I'll write tomorrow or this weekend, I thought to myself over and over. No deadline loomed, so it was easy to push writing to the side. The longer I stayed away from it, the easier it was to justify not finishing what I started. Without a clear purpose for writing, I was not motivated to work on it.

Then, I discovered your *why* is your lifeline out of the Pond of Procrastination. Your *why* cannot be about I! Your *why* is knowing *who* will be positively impacted by what you are doing. Helping others raises your passion for a project. This was affirmed when I heard my friend, Lily Gauthreaux say, "The *how* reveals itself only after the *why* is refined." I had to figure out a way to make this book compliment my business and not compete! I did not want to give up either of them and kept praying for a common thread to pull the two together. Then it hit me, the *why* (the purpose of everything I do) would be to equip women to change the conversations in their heads to change their legacies. I would do this through my business, book, and blog. All platforms would share the same message, only in different forms for different audiences. That was it! I was on fire again, ready to witness the lives changed through erasing and replacing labels.

As soon as the *why* crystallized, I found my editor, the powerful and patient, Michelle Williamson, and Xulon, my publishing company. With a deadline now on the calendar, I was passionately disciplined again and ready to carve out time to write. I did it without sacrificing time from my business. In fact, the process has made my business better, stronger, and more on purpose than any other time in 30 years.

Make a commitment to yourself to stay in motion and obedient to the initial calling even when you can't remember why you started. Promise yourself that you will not quit, settle, or justify even when the process gets boring or hard, and you are not seeing results fast enough.

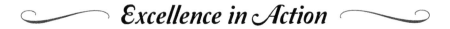

Excellence in Action

👠 What is one project that you have been putting off?

👠 How can it complement what you are currently doing?

👠 Who will be positively impacted when you complete this project?

👠 What is your next best step?

Thoughts Are Holding You Hostage

If you've been living in the Land of Lazy, it is time to wake up and quit lounging around in there. Tie up your sparkly, glitter-covered Tennis Shoes and run from your past—if that is what is keeping you there. Those choices you made were only how you handled a situation, not who you are today! You cannot run in the direction of your dreams if you are being held hostage by guilt and shame. The most oppressive

You cannot run in the direction of your dreams if you are being held hostage by guilt and shame.

chain that keeps us bound and locked in our box, in the Land of Lazy, is the way we process and internalize past choices.

We have all made bad decisions, some of us more than others. On one hand, some choices we believe were bad decisions, while others think they were okay. On the other hand, we view some of the choices we made as okay, while others think they were horrible.

It's so confusing! What matters, of course, is what we believe to be true of our choices. Keep in mind, our past choices were made based on the limited information and experience we possessed at that particular moment in time. Hindsight is always 20/20. We did not know what we did not know. What is so clear today was not even on our radar at the time. We make many choices in life that seem like problem solvers at the time, and later we discover they were some of the worst choices possible. We cannot change them now. The past is gone.

We can change our future. And we can mentor other women to avoid the mistakes we made. We can share our experiences and hope others do not make the same poor choices. Don't let those lousy choices from your past keep you in the box. Don't let embarrassment keep you from sharing your lessons. They were choices, and they had consequences, but they do not determine who you are today unless you give them power over you.

These types of Pitiful labels are some of the worst. We are too embarrassed to share them, so we hide them and feel unworthy. Some of us feel so unworthy that we can't enjoy or embrace healthy relationships or success. We think that people would no longer like or respect us if they knew what we had done. Maybe that's true of some people. If so, wipe them from your mind, and spray yourself with glitter. There isn't enough space for guilt and glitter in the same room.

There isn't enough room for guilt and glitter in the same room.

What are some choices you have allowed to become Pitiful labels in your life?

Excellence in Action

Let's be honest with ourselves and fill in the labels with those choices you have allowed to become your labels. You might need to grab a tissue; this can get a little emotional. Don't hold back. Once you write them down, you change those choices back to an action, not an accusation.

My sweet friend, grab your eraser, get rid of those labels, and replace them with the truth. This is the powerful truth: No one is perfect, and we are doing the best we can. Take the lesson, and throw away the experience. I am very passionate about this lesson. I had an abortion early in life and am now on a mission to let people know the emotional consequences that can come with that choice. I have had the privilege of sharing this story with hundreds of women and young girls. They will make their own choices, but I would have given anything if someone would have told me about the emotional hell that comes with that choice. Because of that abortion, I felt unworthy of a great marriage or great success. This became my label of unworthiness. Fear of judgment by others controlled my actions. What would they say about me? What would they think about my leadership? How would that impact my testimony as a Christian?

Does any of this sound familiar? Let's get real for a minute: The real problem is not their judgment, is it? The voice inside our head is the cruelest and loudest. That is the problem. We are our own worst critic. Would you talk to your best friend the way you talk to yourself? Would you allow your friends to talk to you the way you talk to yourself? Probably not.

Excellence in Action

Take a minute to write out some of those things you say to yourself about yourself that you would never say to someone else:

Now that you have written these down, you will start to recognize them as they arise in your thought life. You are now equipped to erase these negative thoughts about yourself and replace them with Powerful labels. Before long, your new Powerful labels are secure, and the negative self-talk loses its control over your life. As long as these labels swirl around in your head, they have power to create confusion and chaos when you are making decisions.

WHEN LABELS BECOME FILTERS

Did you know a label worn long enough becomes a filter? This filter changes every conversation to match your self-identity. Let's use the filter of unworthiness as an example. When you sift all conversations through this filter, you cannot receive appreciation or admiration. When someone tells you they love or respect you, your second conversation (your filter) blocks it with: *They would not feel that way about me if they knew what I did.* This negative internal response hurts both the giver and receiver in this conversation. The giver can feel your resistance and can become confused about your response. You, as the receiver, can never receive the encouragement you desperately need to move forward in life.

The most dangerous part of this mind exchange is when the conversation shifts from *They would not feel that way about me if they knew "what I did"* to *They would not feel that way about me if they knew "who I was."* When this happens, you have shifted from simply acknowledging that you made a poor choice to the poor choice becoming part of your self-identity. Your view of yourself has become distorted by this filter, so you cannot honestly relate to other people in a healthy way. It is no longer what you did but who you are. You cannot enjoy or experience relationships based on respect because you don't respect yourself. You move from being a victor to becoming a victim.

Excellence in Action

Let me give you some examples of how to Erase and Replace some common phrases from a victim (Pitiful) mentality to a victor (Powerful) mentality and just in case we missed some of your personal favorites, write down a few of the victim phrases you frequently use:

VICTIM	REPLACE	VICTOR
Too busy...		*I'm so blessed to be in demand!*
Overwhelmed...		*Abundantly blessed...*
What if they quit?		*The whole story is not written.*
I can't say no ...		*This is not my best yes during this season of my life.* (Thank you Lysa TerKeurst)

My sweet friend, it is time to draw a line in the sand. Walk away from this internal war waging in your head. The freedom and clarity that comes with forgiving yourself and moving forward is indescribable. You will become powerful beyond words. I know this is true because it took me a long time to forgive myself for that abortion choice I made. When I did, it felt like a two-ton weight had been lifted off of my shoulders. I see now that it was really a two-ton unworthy filter. When you are ready step out of the Land of the Lazy, all you need to do is change your filter to change your future.

Change your filter to change your future.

The improvement in my life was immediate. Intimacy developed in my marriage that was not there previously because I could now receive the love Tom felt for me. My business soared because I no longer had to prove myself through my position on the scoreboard. What a sense of peace to no longer work with a "driven to prove" mentality. Instead, I was able to work with a "called to serve" mentality. It is an amazing difference.

I so want this breakthrough for you. I know your story is different from mine, but the effects are still the same. This is not an overnight fix. You don't have to be perfect from this point forward. You will not get it right all of the time. This is the beauty of being forgiven. Maybe it is time to forgive yourself, and erase the "I am unworthy" label once and for all. Replace it with "I am forgiven," and run out of the Land of the Lazy as fast as you can, so you can excel in the Land of Excellence. It's time to become the Woman of Excellence you were designed to be—all flaws and faults are welcome.

As you take your final step out of the Land of the Lazy, reach back and bring others with you. It is time to speak truth into the lives of those around you. Remind them of their talents, their hopes, and their dreams. Tell them it is not too late to make a course correction. Girlfriend, it is time to stir your soul and awaken those God-ordained dreams. Did you know there are people in your family, in your community, and all around the globe waiting for you to quit being a part of the problem? It is time to quit sitting on the sidelines and beating yourself up. It is time to get involved in the solution. Whether it is donating your time, money, gifts, talents, or vision, you can make a difference by taking one step toward your dream. As my friend Tammy Romage shares, "Remember their dreams are attached to yours." You have friends just lounging around in the Land of the Lazy; love them where they are but don't spend a lot of time with them, or you will find yourself drowning in that Pond of Procrastination. They need you to lead them out. Grab your sparkly Tennis Shoes and sprint out of here, the Land of Excellence is waiting for you!

Women of Excellence

Dr. Lauryn Gilliam, PhD, LMFT

Dr. Lauryn Gilliam and I had lunch one day to talk about the labels associated with infertility. I have been watching many of my friends deal with infertility, and I wanted to learn how to love and support them through this season. My heart was breaking because I was watching powerful women change before my eyes. Once they received the diagnosis, the way they perceived themselves changed from Powerful to Pitiful. I also observed how their friends' reactions to them changed because they did not know how to respond. Here is our interview and I pray it helps you either walk through this season or equips you to walk with someone through this season in a powerful way.

Infertility, we hear about it everywhere we go. Couples invest everything they have to conceive, literally. From their emotional bank to their financial bank, they are spent. Did you know one in eight couples experience infertility issues? These men and women are true warriors; they will not give up or back away. They are all in for the long haul.

Studies show that a diagnosis of infertility for some

has the same emotional trauma as being diagnosed with a terminal illness. The worst part is that the grieving process is every month, not just one time. It affects the entire family, but many times family members are left in the dark because the couple feels too guilty or shameful to share that they can't get pregnant.

Just think about how would you treat anyone with a terminal illness? When you filter your words through this thought, there will be no more judgment and no more avoidance. For those of us walking with our friends through this season, tell them, 'I stand in awe of your commitment.'

People say the wrong things because they don't understand. People assume that you need to take a break, that you are trying too hard to get pregnant; you're over sensitive about it; you're over-focusing on it. They will try to tell you to adopt, take a cruise, or to relax. All of these things insinuate that the couple is doing it wrong or it may be implied that they aren't astute enough to have thought about other possibilities yet. Believe me, they have thought about them, they just aren't ready. Pushing them to explore other options or take a vacation does not make them have an "aha" moment or provide peace. It seems as if the socially constructed idea is that those dealing with infertility issues need to get over it, move on, and "hide the crazy" to keep the rest of us from being uncomfortable.

The labels infertility can cause are numerous and many are self-inflicted. Shame is the root of these Pitiful labels, and they run through all religions and cultures:

☞ You are a failure.

☞ Your God failed you.

☞ Your body failed you.

☞ You are not woman enough to carry a child.

☞ I thought I did everything I was supposed to do.

☞ Everyone thinks I am a Debbie Downer.

Reframe these into Powerful labels:

☞ I am enough.

☞ I can find pleasure in ways other than having a child.

☞ I will reevaluate my purpose to _____ .

☞ My identity is not tied to my ability to have a child, my identity is: _____ .

Many dealing with infertility will find themselves recognizing they have many more talents and abilities than they once believed. The journey creates strength; they're stronger than before the diagnosis. But they can reach this place of peace and loving self-acceptance much quicker with the help of their village. Be a part of a village that lifts people up (Gilliam 2018).

Race To Your Rainboots; It's Time To Maneuver Your Way Out Of The Maze Of Mediocrity

Whew! That was a close call. Now let's peek inside Door #2, the Maze of Mediocrity. Baby, this place is buzzing! It is packed, loud, and full of activity without accomplishment. Like an octopus on roller skates, a lot of movement is going on, but not forward motion. You can find yourself meandering in this maze before you know what happened. It's where the majority of our society lives (halfway between success and failure), and it runs through everything we do, especially the little things when we think no one is looking. For example, you are at the grocery store and have just unloaded your groceries into your car. It is raining, and the cart return is a looooonnnggg way across the parking lot. When you live in the Land of Mediocrity, you just push the cart far enough away from your car to make sure it doesn't cause a scratch or dent. A Woman of Excellence finishes what she starts. She will walk the cart all the way over to the cart stand, or offer it to someone else. I have to tell you, I hear more feedback on this. It is so funny when someone tells me, "I saw you return your cart the other day, I wondered what you were going to do." Whether you know it or not, people are watching you.

I learned this lesson while traveling to Salt Lake City on a business trip. I was so proud of myself—just a wee bit too proud. Swollen as I was with pride, I'm surprised my head made it through the door. Do you have a dress that makes you look tall and skinny? I don't find one often since I am 5'4" and very curvy. But my mentor suggested that I find a more feminine outfit to wear while holding appointments for my business. She thought silk would be just the answer.

At the time, I went to work in a BDU (Battle Dress Uniform) and combat boots. BDU material is starched, and it does not flow at all. No matter how good you feel, in that uniform, your hiney is going to look the size of Texas. So the whole feminine, flowing concept was really fascinating to me. I had only recently stopped using shampoo as my skin care routine and become accustomed to wearing lip gloss and two eyeshadows on a daily basis. That was a lot of "girly" for me. Still, I'm coachable and open to new ideas to be successful. My friends offered to take me shopping and after a full day in the mall, we finally found it….hot pink, flowing, long silk skirt and blazer, and girlfriend, I rocked it. I decided this was the dress to wear on my first out-of-town business trip.

After three productive, successful days, my friend dropped me off at the airport dressed in my flowing hot pink silk suit, and I went into the ladies room. As I left and began to make my way toward my terminal, I noticed several people staring at me. So I lifted my chin, pulled in tummy, and really started to strut. Top runway models had nothing on me. I spied two people nudging each other and thought, *They think I am Nancy McKeon.* (She was a star on the popular '80s TV show *Facts of Life* and I've often been told we resemble one another.) Then it dawned on me that I might need a mint because, as good as I was looking, I just knew there were awesome business connections to be made. As I was buying my mint, a very sweet lady came up behind me and tapped me on the shoulder and whispered in my ear, "Ma'am, your skirt is tucked into your pantyhose." Oh my! It got worse when I remembered I didn't wear panties with my panty hose. I had mooned the entire Salt Lake City airport. People were watching alright. I quickly pulled my skirt out of my panty hose, said thank you very much, and walked the entire length of the airport with my chin down to avoid eye contact.

Keep in mind that people are watching you, good or bad, and when you get a little too full of pride things will happen to bring you back to normal. (By the way, now when I speak at events I always tug at my skirt and drink only water. There is no need to sign up for those lessons again!)

Have you ever had an experience like that? One that left you embarrassed and ashamed? Take the lesson; throw away the experience, and learn to laugh at yourself. You will have many occasions to take full advantage of how funny life can be. Will these experiences make you bitter and keep you in the Maze of Mediocrity or make you better as you step into your dream life as a Woman of Excellence?

Why are so many people in this Maze of Mediocrity? Part of the reason could be the advice they accepted from people when opportunity presented itself. Opportunity will rarely come in a FedEx envelope from God letting you know this is the ticket to your dream life. When opportunity presents itself, it will probably be something you never dreamed you would, could, or should do. However, there is that still small voice that whispers, "You can do it. This is your path out of this maze. Trust me. Don't quit!"

ACCESS THE RIGHT ADVICE

Once your thoughts turn to beginning your dream life journey, you will likely survey other people for opinions on this or that opportunity, charity, ministry, church, etc. Be careful whose advice you take. Remember, most people are choosing Door #2 and meandering in the Maze of Mediocrity. Everyone, including Maze of Mediocrity residents, has an opinion and is willing to steer you in one direction or another. Keep in mind that it's easy for someone to give advice when the consequences aren't theirs to pay. When you are faced with a well-meaning advice giver, ask yourself if this person is financially, spiritually, and emotionally where you want to be. If not, then don't take advice from them. If you are going to go to college, would you talk to a college dropout or a college graduate? If you are planning to get married, are you going to talk to someone who has been married 25 times or 25 years? Everyone runs into the same types of challenges and obstacles. Some people can find a way to work through them and complete what they started, while others justify and find excuses not to finish what they started.

I almost did not start my business because those around me told me every crazy thing they had ever heard about anyone who had ever attempted this type of business. I started my business on a Thursday night, and by Friday I was ready to quit. On Friday morning, I went into my office with great enthusiasm and let them know I was in business! Now keep in mind that, until this point, I did not get along with my coworkers. (This is normal when you put a lot of crabby, broke folks together!) My husband was not excited about my choice because I was already gone about 60 to 70 hours each week. When I was home, I was pretty darn prickly because I was so emotionally, spiritually, and physically exhausted. He also knew how I felt about women, so he said he didn't want me to begin this business. I let him know I had already started my business—so there! (Obviously, I needed more communication skills than I realized.) He reminded me that my language was too colorful for this world of pink. My favorite F-words now are fun, faith, fellowship, but at that time, those were not my go-to F-words. I knew he loved me and really did not care if I started a business or not. He was trying to protect me because I am very gullible. After hearing all of this pushback from my family, my coworkers, and then my man, I was ready to quit.

I can still remember the phone call I made to quit. I was surprised when the tears started to flow, and my heart started to pound out of my chest. I could hear the roar of my thoughts: *What if this is your ticket to get home with Tom and Samantha, so you can be the kind of wife and mom they deserve? What if this is your opportunity to get out of debt? What if this is your way to have a career, lead a ministry, and be at home?* Then it dawned on me, by making this call, I was giving up on the last shred of hope I would ever have of designing and living out my dream life. I would just settle like everyone around me. The message I was intended to share to get women out of the box would never be told. I would live the rest of life just wondering *What if I had tried?*

Connie, my mentor, asked me why was I quitting on myself before I had even tried and asked me who had rained on my parade? I told her all of the pushback I received and she asked me the question that changed the course of my life:

"Will the people who are so quick to give you advice have to pay the consequences for your choice? Will they pay off your debt? Pay your daughter's college tuition? Help with aging parents?"

"Heck no! They can't even pay their own bills!" I told her.

I could hear her smile as she very quietly said: "If you would not trade places with them and they don't have to pay the consequences of your choice, they have not earned the right to give you advice." She went on to say, "Be careful who you take advice from, or you will find yourself living the same life financially, spiritually, and emotionally as they are living right now."

That did it. I committed to giving my business one year of honest effort and committed to becoming a great student. I became part of the "never miss anything club." (That is someone who is at every event and education opportunity.) Within eight months, I had earned the use of my first career car. Guess who was sitting in the front row cheering the loudest? My crazy husband and coworkers! What if I had listened to them? I would not have had the privilege of earning the use of career cars for 29 years! (Eight of the cars have been pink Cadillacs and four pink Escalades) I quickly moved up into a leadership position, and I was earning three times more in my business than I was on active duty and qualified for an early out of the military. I can still feel the freedom of my first day as a work-from-home mom. I can still feel the wind in my hair as I threw my combat boots off the bridge in Omaha, Nebraska that January morning. I still remember the thrill of being there in the afternoon when Samantha got home from preschool. If I had listened to those people, our family would not have benefited from the communication skills that had to be developed to reach this level of success or all of the choices my family enjoyed from the millions in commissions I have earned. This dream life almost did not happen because of someone's advice.

My friend, who are you listening to? Who are you taking advice from? No matter if you tried something before and it did not work, keep trying. Even if you did not finish what you started in the past, you have another shot to live your dream life. Don't let someone else's decisions determine your destiny. Your dream life is just one step out of the box when you choose to listen to the small voice whispering, "You can do this!"

Don't let someone else's decisions determine your destiny.

I wish I could hold your hand right now, look into your eyes, and see the glimmer of hope rising within. The hope shining there proclaims to everyone that you believe your dream life is still there waiting for you. Your dream life won't look like mine; it is your secret treasure to share with the world. Maybe you have already made that call to quit, but it is not too late to restart. It is never too late to begin the journey to living the dream life burning deep in your soul. It is waiting for you behind Door #3. It is time to change out your inner circle (the people you will accept advice from), grab your spray glitter, and leap out of that box.

START STRONG AND FINISH STRONGER

Enough of this storytelling. It's time to get practical. We must make sure we are not choosing Door #2; there is not one darn thing happening there that will help us design our dream life.

Let's start with that "I have tried and failed" label. Trying something that does not work out well does not make you a failure. It makes you smarter. Now you know what doesn't work. Now you are armed with new information that will help you succeed in the future. Take the lesson, and throw away the experience. As you keep trying, you might even find a new passion.

I have had the privilege of leading three different ministries in our church: Guest Experiences, Community Groups, and Missions. Prior to leading these ministries, I had never been in a Community Group or on a mission trip. My only experience was serving as a part of the greeting team. My pastor at the time, Justin Davis, just believed me into leadership. Before this, I never thought I could lead outside of the business world, but thanks to his belief and trust in me, volunteer ministry is now one of my passions. In fact, one thing I now love to do is teach church leaders how to create passion in their volunteer teams with a half-day Ignite workshop. What if I had believed that limiting label: "I cannot teach outside the pink bubble?" (That's a fun nickname I call our Mary Kay world.)

My sweet friend, I wonder if someone asking you to do something outside of your comfort zone? Can you imagine the lives you can impact by getting started today? Just one Be Brave moment is all you need to take that one baby step so you can erase that "I tried and failed" label. Girlfriend! You can do this! Go ahead, put this book down and make that call!

Now that you are feeling stronger, let's pull off the label "You don't finish anything." Start with the small things. Finish the task at hand, and then do "and then some." What is that, you ask? That is doing what is required, and then, just a little more. That extra 1 percent will pay off over time. Just five minutes more of your quiet time gives you a little more than two hours extra each month, and twenty-four hours—a full day—alone in quiet time each year. You will never miss that five minutes, but look at the increase when you do the "and then some." The same thing occurs with exercise, drinking water, work activities, and call lists. Just do one percent more and you can be trusted with more.

The Bible teaches this lesson in the parable of the talents found in Matthew 25:14-30.[21] When you take care of what you have, you will receive more. If you cannot take care of what you have now, what you have will be taken away. Remember, your character is who you are based on the choices you make when no one is looking. It's as my friend Justin Davis shares, "When your giftedness outweighs your character, your mission will implode." The exercises in this book are designed to help you grow your character to match your calling. There is nothing more pathetic than having a small character when you have a big assignment. That is why I constantly pray, "Lord, please give me the growth I can handle today while you continue to grow me into the person who can handle the growth you intend."

We cannot create the future of our dreams as long as yesterday is still impacting our future

We cannot create the future of our dreams as long as yesterday is still impacting our today. Yesterday ended at midnight; you have a clean canvas to design a masterpiece of a day. If you were ready to create a masterpiece painting, would you purchase a dirty canvas? No, you would make sure it was clean, fresh, and smooth. Every morning you get to choose where you start...clean or cluttered. The choices you have made up until today are just part of your story, part of your refining process, so you could grow your character to match your calling. Your story will inspire others because you did not give up, settle, or take advice from the wrong people. It is time to race to your Rain Boots. They will help you in those seasons you find yourself drenched in despair, delay, and discouragement. Believe it or not, "it is all good," and the "whole story is not yet written." Let's do a label Erase and Replace to help you find that rainbow of hope, move out of this maze, and start creating anew.

Excellence in Action

Take a look at what labels are holding you hostage and what labels are equipping you to excel:

PITIFUL	REPLACE	POWERFUL!
I tried and failed.		*I am brave and courageous.*
I don't finish anything.		*"Once I commit I do not quit!"* (Thank you Nancy Boucher for this game changer battle cry!)
I am afraid.		*I am excited for this new adventure.*

Doesn't reading those labels make you feel even more passionate and powerful? I bet your eyebrows rose and you are sitting straighter; I know I am.

Each day we wake up, we decide which of these three doors we will enter. Which one will you choose? If I spent time with you, called your answering machine, or checked your social media posts, I would know which door you are choosing. I heard a pastor share several years ago: "If you want to know where your heart really lies, look in your checkbook and calendar." This is so true. We all invest money and time in what we are most passionate about. Are you spending time watching a TV reality show, or working to make your own dream life a reality?

Are the choices you are making today having an internal, external, and eternal impact in the people you love the most? If not, why waste your time and resources on something that only impacts your bottom line? When this question becomes part of your filter to build a powerful day, you will find your to-do list is much shorter and your energy and expectation much higher!

Excellence in Action

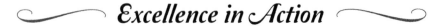 Where are you spending most of your money?

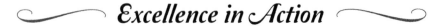 Where are you spending most of your time?

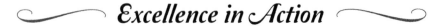 Does this get you closer to your dream life?

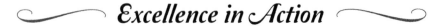 If not, what needs to change?

Another fun thing to do when you decide to step out of the box is to change little things. Voicemail messages are an easy change, and it's fun to see who is paying attention. When you call my office and get my voicemail, here is part of the message you will hear.

"Hi you have reached the office of Diana Sumpter. Sorry, I am not in right now, but I am out changing legacies and helping women design the life they love. Leave a message so I can get back to you. Remember that we

We are too blessed to be stressed, too anointed to be disappointed, and too equipped to be whipped.

are too blessed to be stressed, too anointed to be disappointed, and too equipped to be whipped. Have a miracle-filled day!"

RIVER OF REGRET

Here's the bad news. Crazy as it sounds, many people will try to hold you back, and put those labels right back on you. There are two groups of people who can hold you back: group one wants to protect you from something new, from possible failure, and group two is uncomfortable when you choose excellence over excuses.

This message of mediocrity will only remain true as long as everyone in the maze believes it, and no one proves the message false. Your choice not to believe the "this is as good as it gets" lie forces those around you to take a long hard look at why they are floating around all day in the River of Regret. They have a lot of time invested in this river, and they want you to tread water with them. When you swim out and start living a different life on the shore, they will do whatever it takes to get you back in the water.

I see it all the time. It even has a name: the Crab Syndrome. I lived in Louisiana for twelve years, and I know nothing gets those

Cajuns more excited than a crawfish boil. They put all of the crawfish in a huge barrel without a lid. I once asked a friend why there was nothing on top to keep the crawfish inside the barrel. "They will keep pulling each other back down," he explained "None of them get out." Wow! What a visual for our lives. How many times have we been presented with an escape route and chose not to follow it because the people around us pulled our hopes and dreams down so much that we remained trapped in the maze? Let's make a pact right now that we will neither allow others to hold us back from designing our dream life nor be part of the pack that keeps others from escaping the Maze of Mediocrity.

This Crab Syndrome culture seeps through everything we do. How do you know what culture you are living in? Just listen to words you are speaking. Listen to the words those around you are speaking. Let's listen in:

CULTURE OF QUIT THAT CREATES A PITIFUL LIFE		CULTURE OF COMMITMENT THAT CREATES A POWERFUL LIFE
BREAKDOWN: I don't feel like it.		*BREAKTHROUGH: I love when I have the breakthrough that comes with doing the things I have been unwilling to do.*
SELFISH: I don't want to be inconvenienced.		*SELFLESS: I will do whatever it takes for my people to be successful.*
LAZY: I don't want the responsibility or I want someone else to pay me regardless of how I work.		*LEADER: I want to take control of my paycheck.*
I choose to be a part of the WRECKING CREW. When I go off course it causes others to doubt, since their dreams are attached to mine, I am wrecking the road to both of our dream lives.		*I choose to be part of the BUILDING CREW to equip women how to work through the frustrating times to reach their dream life.*
VICTIM: I don't want the hurt that others have caused.		*VICTOR: I don't take advice from people I would not trade places with financially, spiritually or emotionally.*
COWARD: I will have my people listen to everyone else's training and I teach from theory not experience. I do just enough to SURVIVE and not THRIVE.		*COURAGEOUS: I will do the things that scare me so that I can lead by example. I will choose every day to do one thing I have been unwilling to do. I do the "and then some".*
I work with a SENSE OF ENTITLEMENT. My people owe me respect because of my title or longevity. I thought this was going to be easier, there must be something wrong with my people.		*I work with a SENSE OF GRATITUDE for the privilege to have a platform that allows me to speak powerful truths into the lives of those around me. I focus on WHO I am becoming not just my place on the scoreboard.*

Which words do you need to change to create a culture of commitment in your life?

_____

_____

_____

You may want to take a picture of the commitment side, and put it on your bathroom mirror to read every day. When you choose the Culture of Commitment over the Maze of Mediocrity, you can put those Rain Boots back in the closet. The delays and disappointments no longer have the power to destroy your dreams because you have removed the last of the Pitiful labels, and now you are ready for Door #3.

Women of Excellence

Pamela Waldrop Shaw

Now that you have maneuvered out of that Maze of Mediocrity and you are ready to step into the Land of Excellence, I wanted to show you how Women of Excellence think differently, design their days differently, respond to life differently. They are not immune to the heartbreaks of life, they just choose to continue to pour their hearts into others and passionately peruse their purpose. They are the same whether they are at the bottom or the top of the scoreboard. They fight for what is right whether anyone is looking or not. They are willing to pay the emotional price to make sure the next generation is set up for success. The best example of what this would look like on a daily basis comes from my friend and mentor, Pamela Waldrop Shaw. Here is an excerpt from one of her speeches that is a blueprint to fight for the life you want:

> Live INTENTIONALLY. What entertains you trains you! What you LISTEN to—music, news, sermons, speeches, professors, pastors, mentors, leaders, politicians. What you WATCH—You Tube, Facebook, TV, Netflix, HBO, Snapchat, Instagram, movies. What you READ—Bible, books, articles, posts, magazines, blogs. How you OCCUPY

your TIME—doing nothing, sleeping, eating, overeating, exercising, studying, reading, gaming, serving, working, cleaning, speaking, blogging, google search…HOLDING a party—IT TRAINS your thoughts, formulates beliefs. What entertains you trains you. Period. You can't INPUT one "type" of information and PRINT OUT another. You can't import one form of information and EXPORT another. God is clear. He CREATED US with a BRAIN and with the ability to CHOOSE and to THINK! Mind over matter. We're not victims of our biology or our DNA. His MERCIES are fresh every day. EVERY DAY, new neuron pathways open up to be used for good or for harm. Yours and my thoughts take up valuable mental real estate. They're keeping you in either poverty or wealth in terms of mental wellbeing. Your thoughts are a CHOICE. God created me in HIS image— which is perfect. Made for LOVE, not fear. Sound mind, not insanity. Don't like where this is going? Change what you listen to, what you watch, consume, read, what you do with your time. Watch what follows. You can't LIVE your values until you know what they are! So what would a perfect day be for YOU? Start to finish! Frame your day—the first two hours and last hour—with intentional habits. Those three hours are as critical to your life as the foundation to your home. Nobody is going to turn off the noise or live well for you! ONLY you can. You gotta fight for the life you want to live (Shaw 2018).

HUSTLE INTO YOUR HIGH HEELS; IT'S TIME TO EXCEL IN THE LAND OF EXCELLENCE

Finally, we are at Door #3: the Land of Excellence. This is where Women of Excellence live out loud and cheer each other on to victory. There are no comparison games happening here. In this place, Pitiful labels are not allowed and perfection is not demanded. Here, your little girl dreams have become your big girl reality. Hustle into your High Heels because it is your time to shine as you step into the Land of Excellence. Take a glance over your shoulder at the many people watching you step through the entryway. Their hopes and dreams are connected to your choices. As they watch you be brave and courageous, they believe they can do the same.

When they watch you fight for your thoughts and choose Powerful labels, it inspires them to erase their Pitiful labels and follow you.

You are fearless, my friend, not fear filled. We've probably all heard or read this definition of fear: False Evidence Appearing Real. Fear is the lie that keeps you from opening that door. Inactivity breeds doubt and distrust. Action breeds confidence and courage. If you want to conquer fear, get up and get busy. Don't believe the lie! Reach out your hand, grab that doorknob, and swing the Land of Excellence door wide open!

Inactivity breeds doubt and distrust. Action breeds confidence and courage,

EXCELLING IN THE LAND OF EXCELLENCE

This is it. Door #3 will take you into the life of your dreams; the life you have ardently desired since you were a little girl. It is not crowded in here at all. It is reserved only for those who are passionately pursuing their God-ordained life purpose. No poor Pitiful labels, only Powerful labels proclaiming "This is who I am meant to be" exist here. My sweet friend, here is where you belong. In here, you and other Women of Excellence rub shoulders with the giants of the world. Not necessarily in size or stature, but in passion and purpose.

What is a purpose? Sometimes it is that yearning deep in your heart that screams "Do something about this," or "Make a Difference in this world," or "Change your legacy." Sometimes it is that yearning that makes your heart pound and your imagination go wild with possibilities. It is the reason you were put here on earth. As my friend Trisha Davis explains, "When natural ability meets character, that's when your mission explodes for the good!"

Excellence in Action

Sometimes purpose is not a "change the world" kind of thing; it is simply a lifestyle change. It is refusing to stay the same. It is designing your dream life and making it a reality.

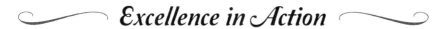 What is the first thing that comes to mind when you think about purpose?

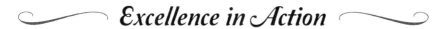 How would you describe your life's purpose to a friend?

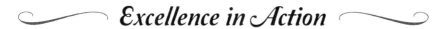 What is one step you could take to discover or design your purpose?

To be a Woman of Excellence, you will need strong daily habits combined with a clear definition of a good day. A good day is different for each of us. It is the choice to complete a small action in each area of our lives every day, whether we feel like it or not. What things need to happen to reach your goals in your faith, your family, and your career? Define what needs to happen to give you a target to shoot for each day. Then, recalibrate your habits to match your goal.

If you don't know what a good day looks like, how will you ever know when to stop or when to stretch? How can you ever celebrate the small daily wins? This is how you grow your self-confidence. Every day that you do what you say you will do, regardless of the results, is a good day. You are evaluating your day based on an activity that you can control. Activity we can control, but the timing of results we cannot. If you are only giving yourself a pat on the back when you reach a tangible goal, there is too much time between the wins. To build a business, a ministry, or a charity, you must close the gap between wins. The more small wins you achieve, the higher your energy and expectations become. When your energy and expectations are high, your attitude and attraction factor skyrocket. When your attitude and attraction skyrocket, resources and results pour in beyond your wildest expectations.

Success is all about momentum, and you can only build momentum by closing the time gaps between your wins. When momentum is present, math ends and magic begins. Normal results don't apply; it is like you have the Midas touch. Everything you touch turns to gold. You can't explain it. It is the power of momentum, and it is a fickle friend. You know it when you have it and know when you don't.

When momentum is present, math ends and magic begins.

S.T.E.P. Into Your Most Powerful Day

The best part about clarifying your good day is that it helps you speak truth into your own life, regardless of what others or the scoreboard says about you. At the end of each day, when you look in the mirror and go over your list, you will either be a Promise Keeper or a Promise Breaker. To put it another way, you are either a Woman of Integrity or you are a Liar. There is no middle ground. You either did what you promised yourself, your family, your colleagues, or your ministry, or you did not. Regardless of how busy you appeared to everyone around you, you did or did not do the tasks that needed to be done to hit your target good day.

You can reprogram your mind to do what you say you will do by imagining what success will feel like at the end of the day when you complete the tasks on your list. When you get to that choice during the day, when you're deciding whether you will do the laundry instead of making calls to your team, think about what that choice will feel like at the end of the day. By thinking through the decision-making process, you get to feel that sense of achievement before it happens, so you make a better choice. The more times you make that good choice, the stronger the habit. With this new habit comes another powerful emotion: peace!

- Peace only happens when you are not controlled by your circumstances or results.

- Peace happens when you are on the right path and making the right decisions.

Peace happens when you know who will be blessed by your daily choices.

Peace comes when success becomes a habit on a daily basis.

WHO AM I?

I am your greatest helper or your heaviest burden. I will push you onward or drag you down to failure. I am completely at your command. Half the things you do you might as well turn over to me and I will be able to do them quickly and correctly. I am easily managed—you must merely be firm with me. Show me exactly how you want something done, and after a few lessons, I will do it automatically.

I am the servant of all great (wo)men and alas, of all failures as well. Those who are great, I have made great, and who are failures, I have made failures. I am not a machine, though I work with all the precision of a machine plus all the intelligence of a (wo)man. You may run me for profit or run me for ruin—It makes no difference to me. Take me, train me, be firm with me and I will place the world at your feet. Be easy with me, and I will destroy you. Who am I? I am a habit. –Unknown

Here is a fun way to create successful daily habits.

Creating a personal S.T.E.P. acronym is a fun way to STEP into your most powerful, purposeful day as a Woman of Excellence:

S stands for savings. Every day make choices that save money, and, if needed, reduce debt. For example, bypass the $5 daily cup of coffee and choose to save the money. This gives you an additional $1,825 dollars a year to deposit into savings, pay down a credit card, or donate to a cause.

T stands for two appointments booked. In my business, holding appointments is necessary to be successful. I strive to have 10 appointments scheduled during the next 10 days so postponements don't impact my peace of mind. Remember, people can only let you down when you lean on them. The more people you have to choose from, the more you can love those who need to step back or go sideways. Keep that can of glitter and your Jesus Filter close by at all times. You need to decide what your activity goal will be for this step.

E stands for emotional. Read at least 10 pages of a good book or listen to a motivational message for ten minutes.

P stands for physical. Make small choices to improve overall physical health: drink eight glasses of water a day, take a brisk 15-minute walk, or choose fruit over a candy bar.

Looked at individually, these small choices may not seem significant, but when you do it every single day it makes a world of difference. For example: When you read daily for 10 minutes, that means you get 70 minutes a week of positive messages. In one month's time, this is more than four hours spent reprogramming your habits, heart, and head. Consider this: eliminate 10 minutes a day of Facebook time for one year and you have 60 hours, that's two-and-one-half days, to be face-to-face with those special people in your life.

Apply this same formula to all four areas and you will see why it is never crowded behind Door #3, while the lands behind Doors #1 and #2 are always jam packed. I really fell in love with this concept after reading Jeff Olson's book *The Slight Edge*[22] and then applied those concepts to my business and life.

Excellence in Action

What will your S.T.E.P. plan include?

S: _____

T: _____

E: _____

P: _____

You will want to come up with your own S.T.E.P. acronym based on whether you are the CEO of your home, the CEO of a multi-million-dollar business, a ministry leader in your church or community, or for us overachievers, all of the above.

Now that you are excelling in the Land of Excellence, we want to make sure you stay here. The life you live tomorrow will be designed by the story you tell about yourself today.

The other day I was driving, and all of a sudden, I started sweating like crazy. I sneezed

The life you live tomorrow will be designed by the story you tell about yourself today.

and thought, *Oh my goodness, I must have a fever.* Then my mind started to race thinking about all the work it would take to change all those appointments. My heart started pounding, and I got even hotter. I began to panic! Then I thought, *Maybe I am not running a fever; maybe I am going through the "change."* All of my friends talk about these hot flashes. *Yes, that must be it.* My mind kept racing, and I started thinking about all the challenges aging will bring into my life.

My shoulders slumped a bit. I looked in the mirror and noticed three new wrinkles, and my hair seemed duller than usual. As my eyes welled up with tears, I looked inside my console to get a tissue and noticed I had turned on the seat heaters. Oh my gracious, I lost 30 minutes of my life because of a darn button. I turned the heaters off, stopped sweating and sneezing, and I swear I looked younger and my hair glistened in the sun. Our thoughts have power. They really do determine how we see ourselves.

Becoming a Woman of Excellence

How you see yourself today determines your ability to passionately pursue your dream life. Your small daily choices are making a much bigger impact on your life than you might realize. You may be doing the same amount of work but are not getting the same results you enjoyed in the past. Take this personal Powerful Me Analysis and you will see that you might have slipped in a few areas. Not a Grand Canyon type of change, just a one-degree pivot away from powerful. These small, seemly insignificant, daily choices impact your energy and expectations, and they can create a totally different experience. Just like doctors testing your heart for a baseline normal so they can recognize when something is off, we are going to do the same with your daily choices. When you have this chart as your baseline for powerful simply analyze and adjust when you feel a little off.

When you were the most powerful version of yourself, what were you doing in these areas of your life?

Excellence in Action

"POWERFUL ME" ANALYSIS

Head

What did you listen to?

Who were you plugging into?

What books did you read?

Where did you post your goal poster and positive affirmations?

What was the message on your voicemail?

Health

When did you work out?

What did you eat to start your day?

What did your food intake look like?

How did you feel in your clothes?

What did you snack on?

Heart

How did this goal move you closer to your dream life?

How were others positively impacted?

Did you create quiet time each day to renew and reflect?

How did your family benefit?

Habits

Did you define a good day, week and month?

How did you track your daily S.T.E.P.?

What other tracking tools were you using?

Help

Did you have a housekeeper?

Did you have office help?

Did you have help with kids?

Did you have virtual help?

Each day you get to decide what you believe about yourself and which labels you will wear throughout the day. Here are five Powerful labels that a Woman of Excellence wears every day (even on those fat, ugly days!)

I will not take advice from people I would not change places with!

~Karen Piro~

I will take "Quit" off the table because once I commit I do NOT quit!

~Nancy Boucher~

I will be a Woman of my Word, especially with the promises I make to myself!

~Diana Sumpter~

I will not let someone else's poor manners affect my future!

~Diana Sumpter~

I will quit trying to change others and work on changing myself!

~Diana Sumpter~

Now, the best part begins. You reach back and pull another woman out of her box and together Erase and Replace her labels. Now, the world is changed forever. In the book *Chase the Lion*[23] by Mark Batterson he reminds us that "Your greatest legacy is not your dream, but the dreams you inspire in others."

There are women in your life who woke up this morning burdened with Pitiful labels, stuck in a box, watching their hopes and dreams diminish day by day. Did you know there is still a small spark just waiting to be ignited?

- Will you be the one who speaks truth into her life, place those Powerful labels on her shoulders, take her hand, and help her step out of the box?

- Will you be the one to fan her dreams, remind her of her purpose, and be her greatest cheerleader?

- Will you be her eyes? Will you tell her all the amazing qualities you see in her?

- Will you teach her how to Erase and Replace the labels in her life?

- Will you partner with her to create a masterpiece that will be her life story?

- Will you give her tools to get started? PS: Don't forget to put that can of glitter in her tool box!

Excellence in Action

Girlfriend, whose dream is being inspired by your life? Who comes to mind? Make a list and call them right away. Fill in their names below.

Go ahead and fill in all of the blanks from the previous chapter so you can see how far you have come during our time together!! Give yourself a hug and a pat on the back!! You did it! Wiggle your toes; you are free from that box!

WHO ARE YOU TAKING WITH YOU? (CHAPTER 8)	WHO CAN YOU EMPOWER? (CHAPTER 4)	PITIFUL LABELS (CHAPTER 2)	POWERFUL LABELS (CHAPTER 2)	DREAM LIFE (CHAPTER 1)
___	___	___	___	___
___	___	___	___	___
___	___	___	___	___
___	___	___	___	___
___	___	___	___	___

Is your heart pounding at the thought of making this kind of eternal, external, and internal impact on another human being? I hope so, that is why we are here, to be the catalyst to ignite the souls of those around us, and through our belief, we get to bridge the gap between Pitiful and Powerful.

This is your mission, should you chose to accept it. We can change the world, and we will do it one woman, one family at a time. Before we know it, an entire community can be changed by the ripple effect of Erasing and Replacing labels. Our homes are changed when the main emotions of hope and possibilities replace discouragement and despair. Lives are changed as women across the globe step bravely out of the box and into their dream life.

Thank you for taking this journey with me. Thank you for investing your time in reading this book. There are so many other things you could be doing. I consider it an honor that you shared these precious moments with me. Now it is your turn to share this message, to put all of this information into action. You might even want to get together for a book study and go through this book together. There is even a free video series and gratitude journal that goes along with this book that will create even more in-depth conversations. Just go to www.dianasumpter.com.

Hustle into your best pair of High Heels, and step out of the box and into the life you were so wonderfully and beautifully designed to live as a Woman of Excellence!

My Commitment As A Woman of Excellence

I am a part of the fellowship of excellence. I have stepped over the line. The decision has been made. I won't give up, shut up, or let up until I have stayed up, stored up, paid up, and prayed up. I won't look back, let up, slow down, back away, or be still.

My past is redeemed; my present makes sense; my future is secure. I am finished and done with low living, colorless dreams, small vision, cheap living, and dwarfed goals. I now live by faith, lean on His presence, labor by power, and lift by prayer.

I cannot be bought, compromised, detoured, lured away, turned back, deluded, or delayed. I will not flinch in the face of sacrifice, hesitate in the presence of fear, negotiate at the table of the enemy, or meander in the Maze of Mediocrity.

From this day forward my banner will be clear. When you see me you will see a Woman of Excellence!

(Adapted from the original poem My Commitment as a Christian, Author Unknown)

-Diana Sumpter © 2012

GRATITUDE JOURNAL

Date:_____

Erase & Replace

I AM GRATEFUL FOR . . .

1. _____

2. _____

3. _____

THE POWERFUL LABELS I WORE WERE . . .

THE PITIFUL LABELS THAT I NEED TO REPLACE . . .

PITIFUL LABEL   REPLACE

PRAYERS   PRAISES

_____   _____
_____   _____
_____   _____
_____   _____

Erase & Replace

I AM GRATEFUL FOR . . .

1. _____

2. _____

3. _____

THE POWERFUL LABELS I WORE WERE . . .

THE PITIFUL LABELS THAT I NEED TO REPLACE . . .

PITIFUL LABEL   REPLACE

PRAYERS   PRAISES

_____   _____
_____   _____
_____   _____
_____   _____

Erase & Replace

I AM GRATEFUL FOR . . .

1. _____

2. _____

3. _____

THE POWERFUL LABELS I WORE WERE . . .

THE PITIFUL LABELS THAT I NEED TO REPLACE . . .

PITIFUL LABEL   REPLACE

PRAYERS   PRAISES

_____   _____

_____   _____

_____   _____

_____   _____

Date:_____

Erase & Replace

I AM GRATEFUL FOR . . .

1. _____

2. _____

3. _____

THE POWERFUL LABELS I WORE WERE . . .

THE PITIFUL LABELS THAT I NEED TO REPLACE . . .

PITIFUL LABEL	REPLACE

PRAYERS	PRAISES
_____	_____
_____	_____
_____	_____
_____	_____

Date:_____

Erase & Replace

I AM GRATEFUL FOR . . .

1. _____

2. _____

3. _____

THE POWERFUL LABELS I WORE WERE . . .

THE PITIFUL LABELS THAT I NEED TO REPLACE . . .

PITIFUL LABEL   REPLACE

PRAYERS   PRAISES

_____   _____

_____   _____

_____   _____

_____   _____

164

Erase & Replace

I AM GRATEFUL FOR . . .

1. _____

2. _____

3. _____

THE POWERFUL LABELS I WORE WERE . . .

THE PITIFUL LABELS THAT I NEED TO REPLACE . . .

PITIFUL LABEL   REPLACE

PRAYERS   PRAISES

_____   _____

_____   _____

_____   _____

_____   _____

Erase & Replace

I AM GRATEFUL FOR . . .

1. _____

2. _____

3. _____

THE POWERFUL LABELS I WORE WERE . . .

THE PITIFUL LABELS THAT I NEED TO REPLACE . . .

PITIFUL LABEL	REPLACE

PRAYERS	PRAISES
_____	_____
_____	_____
_____	_____
_____	_____

Erase & Replace

I AM GRATEFUL FOR . . .

1. _____
2. _____
3. _____

THE POWERFUL LABELS I WORE WERE . . .

THE PITIFUL LABELS THAT I NEED TO REPLACE . . .

PITIFUL LABEL	REPLACE

PRAYERS

_____
_____
_____
_____

PRAISES

_____
_____
_____
_____

Date:_____

Erase & Replace

I AM GRATEFUL FOR . . .

1. _____

2. _____

3. _____

THE POWERFUL LABELS I WORE WERE . . .

THE PITIFUL LABELS THAT I NEED TO REPLACE . . .

PITIFUL LABEL   REPLACE

PRAYERS   PRAISES

_____   _____

_____   _____

_____   _____

_____   _____

Date:_____

Erase & Replace

I AM GRATEFUL FOR . . .

1. _____
2. _____
3. _____

THE POWERFUL LABELS I WORE WERE . . .

THE PITIFUL LABELS THAT I NEED TO REPLACE . . .

PITIFUL LABEL   REPLACE

PRAYERS   PRAISES

_____   _____
_____   _____
_____   _____
_____   _____

Date:_____

Erase & Replace

I AM GRATEFUL FOR . . .

1. _____

2. _____

3. _____

THE POWERFUL LABELS I WORE WERE . . .

THE PITIFUL LABELS THAT I NEED TO REPLACE . . .

PITIFUL LABEL   REPLACE

PRAYERS   PRAISES

_____   _____

_____   _____

_____   _____

_____   _____

Date:_____

Erase & Replace

I AM GRATEFUL FOR . . .

1. _____

2. _____

3. _____

THE POWERFUL LABELS I WORE WERE . . .

THE PITIFUL LABELS THAT I NEED TO REPLACE . . .

PITIFUL LABEL   REPLACE

PRAYERS   PRAISES

_____   _____
_____   _____
_____   _____
_____   _____

Erase & Replace

I AM GRATEFUL FOR . . .

1. _____

2. _____

3. _____

THE POWERFUL LABELS I WORE WERE . . .

THE PITIFUL LABELS THAT I NEED TO REPLACE . . .

PITIFUL LABEL	REPLACE

PRAYERS	PRAISES
_____	_____
_____	_____
_____	_____
_____	_____

Date:_____

Erase & Replace

I AM GRATEFUL FOR . . .

1. _____
2. _____
3. _____

THE POWERFUL LABELS I WORE WERE . . .

THE PITIFUL LABELS THAT I NEED TO REPLACE . . .

PITIFUL LABEL   REPLACE

PRAYERS   PRAISES

_____   _____
_____   _____
_____   _____
_____   _____

Erase & Replace

I AM GRATEFUL FOR . . .

1. _____

2. _____

3. _____

THE POWERFUL LABELS I WORE WERE . . .

THE PITIFUL LABELS THAT I NEED TO REPLACE . . .

PITIFUL LABEL   REPLACE

PRAYERS   PRAISES

_____   _____

_____   _____

_____   _____

_____   _____

Date:_____

Erase & Replace

I AM GRATEFUL FOR . . .

1. _____

2. _____

3. _____

THE POWERFUL LABELS I WORE WERE . . .

THE PITIFUL LABELS THAT I NEED TO REPLACE . . .

PITIFUL LABEL	REPLACE

PRAYERS

PRAISES

_____   _____

_____   _____

_____   _____

_____   _____

Date:_____

Erase & Replace

I AM GRATEFUL FOR . . .

1. _____

2. _____

3. _____

THE POWERFUL LABELS I WORE WERE . . .

THE PITIFUL LABELS THAT I NEED TO REPLACE . . .

PITIFUL LABEL   REPLACE

PRAYERS   PRAISES

_____   _____

_____   _____

_____   _____

_____   _____

Erase & Replace

I AM GRATEFUL FOR . . .

1. _____
2. _____
3. _____

THE POWERFUL LABELS I WORE WERE . . .

THE PITIFUL LABELS THAT I NEED TO REPLACE . . .

PITIFUL LABEL   REPLACE

PRAYERS   PRAISES

_____   _____
_____   _____
_____   _____
_____   _____

Erase & Replace

I AM GRATEFUL FOR . . .

1. _____

2. _____

3. _____

THE POWERFUL LABELS I WORE WERE . . .

THE PITIFUL LABELS THAT I NEED TO REPLACE . . .

PITIFUL LABEL	REPLACE

PRAYERS	PRAISES
_____	_____
_____	_____
_____	_____
_____	_____

Date:_____

Erase & Replace

I AM GRATEFUL FOR . . .

1. _____

2. _____

3. _____

THE POWERFUL LABELS I WORE WERE . . .

THE PITIFUL LABELS THAT I NEED TO REPLACE . . .

PITIFUL LABEL   REPLACE

PRAYERS   PRAISES

_____   _____

_____   _____

_____   _____

_____   _____

Erase & Replace

I AM GRATEFUL FOR . . .

1. _____

2. _____

3. _____

THE POWERFUL LABELS I WORE WERE . . .

THE PITIFUL LABELS THAT I NEED TO REPLACE . . .

PITIFUL LABEL	REPLACE

PRAYERS	PRAISES
_____	_____
_____	_____
_____	_____
_____	_____

Erase & Replace

I AM GRATEFUL FOR . . .

1. _____

2. _____

3. _____

THE POWERFUL LABELS I WORE WERE . . .

THE PITIFUL LABELS THAT I NEED TO REPLACE . . .

PITIFUL LABEL	REPLACE

PRAYERS	PRAISES
_____	_____
_____	_____
_____	_____
_____	_____

Erase & Replace

I AM GRATEFUL FOR . . .

1. _____

2. _____

3. _____

THE POWERFUL LABELS I WORE WERE . . .

THE PITIFUL LABELS THAT I NEED TO REPLACE . . .

PITIFUL LABEL	REPLACE

PRAYERS

_____

_____

_____

_____

PRAISES

_____

_____

_____

_____

Erase & Replace

I AM GRATEFUL FOR . . .

1. _____

2. _____

3. _____

THE POWERFUL LABELS I WORE WERE . . .

THE PITIFUL LABELS THAT I NEED TO REPLACE . . .

PITIFUL LABEL	REPLACE

PRAYERS	PRAISES
_____	_____
_____	_____
_____	_____
_____	_____

Date:_____

Erase & Replace

I AM GRATEFUL FOR . . .

1. _____

2. _____

3. _____

THE POWERFUL LABELS I WORE WERE . . .

THE PITIFUL LABELS THAT I NEED TO REPLACE . . .

PITIFUL LABEL	REPLACE

PRAYERS

_____

_____

_____

_____

PRAISES

_____

_____

_____

_____

Date:_____

Erase & Replace

I AM GRATEFUL FOR . . .

1. _____

2. _____

3. _____

THE POWERFUL LABELS I WORE WERE . . .

THE PITIFUL LABELS THAT I NEED TO REPLACE . . .

PITIFUL LABEL	REPLACE

PRAYERS	PRAISES
_____	_____
_____	_____
_____	_____
_____	_____

Erase & Replace

I AM GRATEFUL FOR . . .

1. _____

2. _____

3. _____

THE POWERFUL LABELS I WORE WERE . . .

THE PITIFUL LABELS THAT I NEED TO REPLACE . . .

PITIFUL LABEL	REPLACE

PRAYERS	PRAISES
_____	_____
_____	_____
_____	_____
_____	_____

Date:_____

Erase & Replace

I AM GRATEFUL FOR . . .

1. _____

2. _____

3. _____

THE POWERFUL LABELS I WORE WERE . . .

THE PITIFUL LABELS THAT I NEED TO REPLACE . . .

PITIFUL LABEL   REPLACE

PRAYERS   PRAISES

_____   _____

_____   _____

_____   _____

_____   _____

Date:_____

Erase & Replace

I AM GRATEFUL FOR . . .

1. _____
2. _____
3. _____

THE POWERFUL LABELS I WORE WERE . . .

THE PITIFUL LABELS THAT I NEED TO REPLACE . . .

PITIFUL LABEL   REPLACE

PRAYERS   PRAISES

_____   _____
_____   _____
_____   _____
_____   _____

Date:_____

Erase & Replace

I AM GRATEFUL FOR . . .

1. _____
2. _____
3. _____

THE POWERFUL LABELS I WORE WERE . . .

THE PITIFUL LABELS THAT I NEED TO REPLACE . . .

PITIFUL LABEL   REPLACE

PRAYERS   PRAISES

_____   _____
_____   _____
_____   _____
_____   _____

Thank You From the Top of my Glitter Covered Head to the Bottom of my High Heeled Feet!

Many thanks to those who held my hand as I stepped out of the box! This has been a three and half year labor of love. There are so many who have poured belief and wisdom into this project; there is no way I could have done this on my own.

Thank you, Lord, for this burning desire to share this "step out of the box" message with women all around the world. Thank you for the words You placed on my heart that showed up with such clarity in this book. It is such a privilege to speak truth into the lives of women and give them the tools to defeat the lies that are constantly whispered in their ears.

Thank you to the love of my life, my husband, Tom, for your patience with my passion to share this message with so many people. What a blessing to have a husband who encourages me to chase after my dreams and not to settle for someone else's definition of a dream life! My dream life began the day I saw you playing volleyball in those blue shorts with the yellow stripe, and my heart still skips a beat when you walk in the room. I am honored to be your wife. I am so glad you picked me 35 years ago.

Thank to our daughter, Samantha, for your constant encouragement! This book would not have been finished without your excitement and vision. Every time I would quit thinking about the message that needed to be shared, you reminded me of my calling. Your dad and I are so blessed you are our daughter. What a joy to watch you be such an amazing and fabulous mom to Dakota.

Thanks so much to our granddaughter, Dakota, who has inspired me to write because she has already written five books and she is only 13! I cannot wait to see what God is going to do in your life sweet girl; I know it is going to be spectacular!

Thank you to my sister, Donna Brewington, who has always been more like a mom than a sister, and as we grow older, what a blessing it is that we choose to be friends instead of just family. Your unwavering belief in me fuels me when those Pitiful labels come out to play. Thank you for being my proofreader extraordinaire!

Thank you Jea Gackowski, Jenn Garton, Melissa Leger, Sami Cone, and Jessica Hardy for all the time you invested coaching me on the process of pulling this book out of my head and putting it on paper. I so appreciate all of the time and red ink it took together to create this final manuscript.

Thank you to Karen Piro and Connie Lamp my friends and greatest cheerleaders. I am the woman I am today because of your mentorship and example. Thank you for pouring into this rough-edged Air Force girl and helping me to uncover the woman I really was designed to be.

Thank you to my sweet mom and dad; you gave me roots of unconditional love and wings of unwavering belief. Thank you for allowing me to be me, even when it did not make any sense!

Thank you to Debbie Jessee for all the work you have done in my office along with creating these amazing graphics. Pictures can explain a concept better than any set of words. I so appreciate you working so hard to make this message clear to so many. Labels will be recognized and Erased and Replaced because of the pictures you created. I am so thankful the Lord placed you in my life at "such a time as this." You made this final push to the finish line so much fun.

Thank you Lacie Williams for creating my mini-me avatar. She is just as curvy as I am! Your belief in me encouraged me to be brave enough to even entertain the thought of writing this book.

Thank you to my editor, Michelle Williamson, for all of your work to clean up the writing so together we can equip women to step out of the box. The lives and legacies that will be changed because of the lessons in this book happened because you kept me focused on finishing strong! You most definitely have the patience of Job to work with us first-time authors!

Thank you to Xulon Publishing for taking a chance on this first-time author and creating a support staff of enthusiastic people who are almost as excited about this book as I am!

Thank you to my "*Lion Chaser* Girlfriends" Weslee, Esther, Brandy, Hannah, Amber, Niki, Mariah and Margaret, I love how we encourage each other to Erase and Replace the thoughts that stand in way of our God-ordained purpose. My life is much richer because of our Thursday morning Bible study!

To my newest friend, YOU!! Your time is your most valuable commodity, so the fact you are investing a part of your life to read this book humbles me beyond words. Thank you for trusting me enough to take this journey together to step you into your dream life. Thank you for being bold enough to uncover that Woman of

Excellence hidden deep inside who is ready to come out and make her mark on this world. Who would have ever thought a pair of high heels could be so powerful! As you walk into your Land of Excellence may you find your greatest love, greatest friends, and choose to be the greatest version of yourself!!

CONTACT THE AUTHOR

To learn more about Diana Sumpter, please visit:
www.dianasumpter.com

REFERENCES

1. Kris and Tim Hallbom, "Exploring the Neuroscience and Magic Behind Setting Your Intent – And Creating an Optimal Future for Yourself," http://www.nlpca.com/creating-an-optimal-future-for-yourself.html

2. Napoleon Hill, "Think and Grow Rich", (Official Publication of the Napoleon Hill Foundation; Sound Wisdom; Original First Edition 1937 edition)

3. Philippians 4:8, (Holy Bible, New International Version®, NIV® Copyright ©1973, 1978, 1984, 2011 by Biblica, Inc.® Used by permission. All rights reserved worldwide.)

4. Brian Tracy, "Making Course Corrections" https://www.briantracy.com/blog/brians-words-of-wisdom/making-course-corrections

5. Erase & Replace Journal, by Diana Sumpter, September 2017, www.dianasumpter.com

6. Donald O. Clifton and Paula Nelson, "Soar with Your Strengths: A Simple Yet Revolutionary Philosophy of Business and Management", (Published 2002 by Dell Publishing)

7. Simon Sinek: You Tube video "Start with Why"

8. "The Roman Road to Salvation" 1) Romans 3:23, 2) Romans 3:10, 3) Romans 5:12, 4) Romans 6:23, 5) Romans 5:8, 6) Romans 10:9-10, 7) Romans 10:13, 8) Romans

10:17, (Holy Bible, New International Version®, NIV®
Copyright ©1973, 1978, 1984, 2011 by Biblica, Inc.® Used
by permission. All rights reserved worldwide.)

9.   Esther 4:14, (Holy Bible, New International Version®,
NIV® Copyright ©1973, 1978, 1984, 2011 by Biblica, Inc.®
Used by permission. All rights reserved worldwide.)

10. Queen of the Channel®, http://www.queenofthechannel.
com/florence-chadwick

11. "The Ivy Lee Method Is The 100-Year-Old Productivity
Secret", https://curiosity.com/topics/the-ivy-lee-method-
is-the-100-year-old-productivity-secret-curiosity/

12. Women Financial Statistics, September 16, 2017, http://
www.statisticbrain.com/women-financial-statistics/

13. Emmie Martin, "Here's how much American women
earn at every age", September 12, 2017, https://www.cnbc.
com/2017/09/12/heres-how-much-money-american-
women-earn-at-every-age.html

14. Elyssa Kirkham, "1 in 3 Americans Has Saved $0
for Retirement", March 14, 2016, http://time.com/
money/4258451/retirement-savings-survey/

15. The average college debt ranges from $60,000-$80,000
with monthly payments around $1,000 a month (Success
magazine) Sarah Landrum, "The Impact of Student Loan
Debt on the Millennial Happiness", October 20, 2017,
https://www.forbes.com/sites/sarahlandrum/2017/10/20/

the-impact-of-student-loan-debt-on-millennial-happiness/#400301577125

16. Zach Friedman, "Student Loan Debt in 2017", https://www.forbes.com/sites/zackfriedman/2017/02/21/student-loan-debt-statistics-2017/#4ec69995daba

17. Erin ElIssa, "2016 American Household Credit Card Debt Study", https://www.nerdwallet.com/blog/average-credit-card-debt-household/

18. Elaine Pofeldt, "Intuit: On-Demand Workers Will More Than Double by 2020", August 2015, https://www.forbes.com/sites/elainepofeldt/2015/08/13/intuit-on-demand-workers-will-more-than-double-by-2020/#160527bdc460

19. Mark Twain, https://www.goodreads.com/quotes/646569-find-a-job-you-enjoy-doing-and-you-will-never

20. Kenoly, Ron. "Ancient of Days." Integrity Music. 2013. CD.

21. Matthew 25:14-30: "Again, it will be like a man going on a journey, who called his servants and entrusted his wealth to them.

To one he gave five bags of gold, to another two bags, and to another one bag, each according to his ability. Then he went on his journey.

The man who had received five bags of gold went at once and put his money to work and gained five bags more.

So also, the one with two bags of gold gained two more.

But the man who had received one bag went off, dug a hole in the ground and hid his master's money.

"After a long time the master of those servants returned and settled accounts with them.

The man who had received five bags of gold brought the other five. 'Master,' he said, 'you entrusted me with five bags of gold. See, I have gained five more.'

"His master replied, 'Well done, good and faithful servant! You have been faithful with a few things; I will put you in charge of many things. Come and share your master's happiness!'

"The man with two bags of gold also came. 'Master,' he said, 'you entrusted me with two bags of gold; see, I have gained two more.

"His master replied, 'Well done, good and faithful servant! You have been faithful with a few things; I will put you in charge of many things. Come and share your master's happiness!

"Then the man who had received one bag of gold came. 'Master,' he said, 'I knew that you are a hard man, harvesting where you have not sown and gathering where you have not scattered seed.

So I was afraid and went out and hid your gold in the ground. See, here is what belongs to you.'

"His master replied, 'You wicked, lazy servant! So you knew that I harvest where I have not sown and gather where I have not scattered seed?

Well then, you should have put my money on deposit with the bankers, so that when I returned I would have received it back with interest.

"'So take the bag of gold from him and give it to the one who has ten bags.

For whoever has will be given more, and they will have an abundance. Whoever does not have, even what they have will be taken from them.

And throw that worthless servant outside, into the darkness, where there will be weeping and gnashing of teeth.', (Holy Bible, New International Version®, NIV® Copyright ©1973, 1978, 1984, 2011 by Biblica, Inc.® Used by permission. All rights reserved worldwide.)

22. Jeff Olson, "The Slight Edge: Turning Simple Disciplines Into Massive Success", (Published May 2011 by Success Books)

23. Mark Batterson, "Chase The Lion", (Published 2016 by The Fedd Agency, Inc.)